# Beyond
# The
# Headset
# Finding My Voice

Kris Ella Crawford

# DEDICATION

For every dispatcher who has ever carried the weight of silence, and for every voice that reminded us we are never truly alone.

# CONTENTS

# ACKNOWLEDGMENTS

Writing this book was not a solo journey. It was born out of years of survival, the echoes of countless calls, and the voices of people who believed in me when I had nothing left to give.

To my daughters, you were raised by the broken parts of me, the versions of me stitched together by survival rather than healing. And somehow, you still grew into women with more light, strength, and grace than I had to give at the time. I know those fractured pieces shaped your childhood in ways I can't undo. Kayla, even if you can't hear this right now, I carry the weight of what you feel. And Linda, thank you for staying close as I work through the pieces I should've faced years ago. You both came from the same storm, even if your paths split in different directions. I love you both, in the silence, in the space between us, in every version of who we've been. And I'll keep doing the work, not to earn forgiveness, but because you deserved a whole mother, not a fractured one.

To Luther, my husband, my anchor, thank you for being the calm after the storm. You loved me in the places I thought were too broken to be seen. Your patience and faith helped me find my way back to myself.

To my mom and my sisters, for standing beside me through battles I never thought I could face, and for never letting me forget that our voices matter.

To Jeff Slapp (Retired Captain) and every mentor who pushed me, believed in me, and taught me how to lead with both strength and compassion, your influence will always be felt in my work.

To my dispatch family, those who sat beside me through the hardest seasons, who witnessed the human cost of this work and offered understanding instead of judgment, you are the invisible strength of this profession.

To Denise Amber Lee, whose 2008 case reshaped how we train, how we listen, and how we teach others to hear what isn't said, your legacy lives in every classroom and every quiet moment behind a headset.

Thank you to everyone who held space for me, believed in me, and gave me the courage to speak. This is just as much yours as it is mine.

# CHAPTER 1

## WHEN SAFETY HAD A PORCH

In the late 1970s, Sarasota, Florida, was a place that clung to you. The heat lay over everything like a heavy quilt. The air carried the sticky-sweet perfume of orange blossoms, tangled with the slow, hypnotic hum of cicadas that never seemed to tire. In a tiny white house on 13th Street with rattling jalousie windows, my sister Carol and I reigned over our little kingdom. Always alert to the slightest changes in the air, a skill I didn't know I'd one day use to read the voices of strangers in their worst moments.

We tore barefoot across sunburned grass. Our skin salted from hours outside, our hair a wild, tangled banner in the breeze. My bike was green, with a glittery banana seat that caught the light like shards of crushed glass; hers was blue, the handlebars worn smooth by her grip. We carved crooked loops through the backyard and collapsed in the sandbox to build lopsided castles that leaned as if they were tired, too. Back then, the only deadlines we knew were the call to dinner, nothing like the ticking clock that would one day dictate every second of my work.

The house was cloaked in shadows, the air thick and unmoving. The box fan that would later remind me of the low hum of a computer room, turning the warm air in lazy circles while we lay under thin Sesame Street sheets, our legs sticking to the fabric. The windows

1

clattered when the wind picked up, and the smell of dinner, maybe meatloaf or fried bologna, would drift from the kitchen, pulling us back inside from our dusty adventures.

It wasn't much by anyone's standards, with no air conditioning and no luxuries, but in our world, we had everything that mattered: each other, endless afternoons, and a backyard that felt like it went on forever.

Our father was more shadow than man, slipping in and out of our lives without explanation. His visits were brief flickers of light, quickly followed by long stretches of darkness. Each time he left, the absences grew longer, his returns less frequent. My mother, Linda, did her best to anchor us, holding together the loose threads of stability with her own weary hands. She rose before dawn, the sky still ink-black, to run her paper route. When she came back, her fingers were cool from the morning air and smelled faintly of newsprint. She'd set a pot on the stove and stir cream of wheat until it thickened, then dust it with sugar that melted into little pools of sweetness.

She hummed gospel songs as she worked, soft, steady notes learned from her grandmother, Mamaw Roxie, who lived with us then. She used to take us to Disney World every weekend before she got sick. The mornings weren't filled with her chatter anymore. Now her quiet presence was an anchor, a reminder that some things, however small, could be relied on. My mother's love was like that, unassuming, almost shy. It didn't announce itself in grand gestures. But in the way she made sure we were fed, in the freedom she gave us to roam barefoot until dusk, in the roof she kept over our heads, no matter how thin the walls.

Even as a child, I sensed something missing from her eyes, a hollow space where tenderness should have lived, left empty by its absence in her own upbringing. She was raising us from scraps, reading subtle cues, a skill I'd later use in dispatch, piecing together affection from what little she had been given, stitching it into something that might hold.

Nana was my mom's mother, my grandmother, a woman with eyes like shuttered windows and a voice that rarely softened. She wasn't unkind, exactly, just unreachable, as if tenderness were a language she'd never been taught. With my mother, love revealed itself through

2

criticism disguised as guidance, a constant pointing toward what might have been done better, what wasn't quite enough. Praise was scarce, and approval even scarcer.

My mother grew up learning to chase affection that seldom arrived, and that absence shaped how she loved us, quietly, cautiously, as though too much softness might dissolve the moment you reached for it. Nana's coldness was a generational inheritance, passed down like an heirloom of restraint, one I carried as well, until the headset demanded otherwise.

The safest place I knew was Paw Paw's house. He was tall and lanky, a World War II veteran whose eyes squinted as if he'd spent a lifetime studying horizons, reading the weather before anyone else could. His hands were calloused yet gentle, the kind that could mend a fence in the morning and peel an orange for you in the afternoon without tearing a single thread of rind. When he hugged you, it wasn't a polite pat on the back; it was an anchoring, a full pull into his chest, his arms locking around you as if to say, You're mine, you're safe, you belong.

But safety like that never lasted. It could vanish with a single phone call, a slammed door, or a decision made without you. One season, I was peeling oranges in his kitchen; the next, I was learning how quickly calm could unravel into chaos.

The air inside carried the scent of bacon grease and old wood, mingled with the faint musk of quilts that had weathered decades of winters. It was the smell of mornings without hurry, of a place that had nothing to prove. Sometimes he'd let me "help" him fry eggs, steadying my small hand with his big one as I tried to flip them without breaking the yolk. Lunch might be a cold hot dog straight from the fridge, or a Milky Way bar that clung to your teeth until you had to pry it loose with your tongue.

We'd sprawl belly-down on the thick gold-brown shag carpet, watching Hee Haw reruns flicker across the TV as the old box fan hummed from the corner, Paw Paw chuckling softly at the same jokes he'd heard a hundred times.

It wasn't magic, exactly; nothing sparkled or shimmered. But it was steady. Gentle. Predictable. And for a kid like me, who never knew when the ground might shift beneath her feet, that steadiness was the purest form of love.

But the stillness of those weekends at Paw Paw's stood in sharp, almost jarring contrast to life at home. My mother's new marriage to my stepfather turned our lives into a restless carousel of new military addresses and recycled promises, from Norfolk's salty harbor air to San Diego's dry heat to Corpus Christi's sticky Gulf winds. Each move was framed as a fresh start, but the turbulence always traveled with the dishes and linens, settling into the walls before we'd even finished unpacking. Stability stayed just out of reach, as if we were chasing it across the map.

My stepfather drank heavily, and when he did, his moods could shift quickly and unpredictably. What I witnessed were arguments behind closed doors, the kind that made the air feel charged long before I could hear words. I experienced fear in that home. I learned to read the air like a storm front, scanning for danger, watching for the slow slur of his words, the unsteady sway in his stance, the acrid-sweet smell of whiskey that clung to him and told me trouble was already in the room.

My older sister, Carol, who had experienced trauma and sexual abuse, began to show signs of it in ways no one could name or fix, in explosions of anger and long silences that made the air itself feel heavy. And me? I became the ghost in my own story. I learned early that safety could sometimes be bought with silence, that if I kept my head down and made myself small enough, maybe I could slip beneath the radar. Invisibility became my armor, my breath.

He punished me in ways that felt theatrical and degrading, like making me run in place, holding heavy frying pans until my shoulders burned. In those moments, it felt less like discipline and more like he needed to dominate the room. That's how I interpreted it as a child. Sometimes we would go for a hike, and he would take off quickly, leaving us behind. As a child, it *felt* like abandonment, like he was testing how far he could push us before we broke. He would fade into the distance, leaving only the hum of cicadas, the rustle of unseen animals, and the thick, damp smell of the woods pressing close.

That's where I first learned to disappear, not with my feet but in my mind. I built a safe room inside myself, quiet and untouched, a place no one else could enter. It became my refuge when his voice rose and anger filled the walls. My stepfather would lean down, his finger jabbing at my forehead, shouting, "Is anyone in there?" while my sister yelled, "Leave her alone," and I stood frozen, waiting for it to end. But I was already gone. I had slipped into the silence, into the one place he could never follow.

That skill, retreating inward, kept me alive back then. But survival habits tend to follow you long after the danger has passed. Years later, during arguments in my marriages, I would disappear in the same way, go quiet, eyes open but mind far away, retreating to that same mental hiding place. What once protected me as a child began to harm me as an adult. Silence had saved me, but it also took away my voice.

Love in our house had no fixed shape. It could be warm in the morning, laughing over breakfast, and turn sharp-edged by nightfall. It didn't take much for tenderness to twist into punishment, and I learned to read the air the way sailors read the sky, scanning for storms before they broke.

My biological father was more of a shadow than a parent. He drifted in and out of our lives, showing up with promises of ice cream or a trip to the park, only to take us across state lines without permission. It wasn't just once or twice; it happened again and again. He framed those trips as visitation. But they happened without notice and without my mother's knowledge. As a child, it felt like being taken, suddenly, jarringly, pulled out of our world and into his.

On one of those trips, in a sweltering Florida campground, he sexually touched my body. I remember freezing, lungs tight, not knowing how to move. Later, he muttered an apology. I experienced it as hollow and dismissive, as if he expected the moment to vanish if he named it lightly. I couldn't name what he'd done, but the disgust lodged deep, taking root in a place I wouldn't uncover for years.

5

He had us call my mother from payphones, pretending everything was normal. That's how it felt to me, like we were performing a script. I watched him dial, memorized each number, and burned it into my mind like a survival code. I didn't know when, but I knew I'd need it.

One day at the public pool, he dropped us off as if we were just kids out for a swim. But as his car disappeared, I tightened my grip on my little sister's hand and led her past the chain-link fence, straight to the payphone. My heart pounded so hard I thought it might drown out the dial tone. With trembling fingers, I dialed the numbers I'd memorized, each one a lifeline.

When my mother's voice came through, I didn't waste time. I told her where we were and that we needed her. That moment, standing on hot pavement, clutching my younger sister's hand, whispering into a payphone, was the first time I saved us. His actions changed the trajectory of my childhood in ways I didn't have the language for at the time. Somewhere inside the silence he forced on me, there was still a voice. And it found a way out.

Looking back, I can see the pieces connect: kidnappings, sexual abuse, punishments that blurred the line between care and cruelty, and fleeting kindnesses that made me ache for more of what I rarely got. Yet scattered among the wreckage are the threads I still hold onto, Paw Paw's laugh, the grit of sand between my toes, and the green shimmer of my bike seat in the sun. Those moments remind me that even in the deepest dysfunction, some part of me still believed in love. Maybe that belief, fragile as it was, carried me through.

Leaving didn't end the abuse; it just redirected it. After I got out, my younger sister Kelly became the target. She carried the violence I escaped. She was buried in dirt, smothered with paint thinner, and had pills shoved down her throat. I didn't learn the full extent of it until years later, sitting in a courtroom as she testified while he pled the Fifth, hiding behind silence because the truth would have damned him.

And when she was sent to live with my biological father, the cycle didn't break; it repeated itself. He did to her what he once did to me. Different house, same nightmare.

The brutality she endured is hard to put into words. But the part that cuts the deepest is simple: the wounds came from the men we were taught to trust. The ones we were told to call "father" and "stepfather." The ones who should've protected us and instead became the reason we needed protection.

That constant traumatic snatching, that's what it was, didn't just disrupt our lives; it rewired how we understood the world. It made chaos feel normal. Made instability look routine. And when you teach a child that kidnapping and abuse are just another version of love, something in them breaks.

It's sick, the kind that doesn't leave bruises but carves scars all the same.

From my vantage point as a child, those removals felt sudden and without warning, as if we could be moved on a whim, like objects rather than daughters. No regard for the trauma, no care for the courts, no concern for the wreckage left behind.

I still carry anger, not just at him but at how impossible it felt, back then, to get adults to truly see what was happening in our world. Everything was labeled 'complicated,' and as a child, it made me feel unseen and unprotected.

Maybe the cruelest part was how he dressed it up as love, as if unpredictability were affection, as if being taken without warning were some fatherly gesture. As a child, I almost believed him. That's what children do. We try to make sense of the senseless. We tell ourselves, At least he came for us.

But now I know better. He took us, and looking back, it felt like it was about his needs, not ours.

That realization still stings, even now. Because I'm still unlearning the lies he taught me: that love is unpredictable, that safety is temporary, that people can disappear without warning, and that you have to accept it.

But I won't pretend anymore. I won't soften it to protect him or his memory. Every time he drove off with us without my mother's knowledge, every time he shrugged off the harm with a weak apology, I lost another piece of trusting the world. And I'm done calling that love.

I was young and naive when I married my first husband. At first, his attention felt like rescue, like someone finally choosing me. Over time, I experienced sudden shifts: slammed doors, objects thrown, tension that escalated fast. When I became pregnant with our first child, Kayla, I thought fatherhood might change him. Instead, the drinking worsened. Nights blurred into arguments in crowded bars, his voice sharp, his hands rough. Six months pregnant, exhausted and swollen, I remember reaching for the door to leave. In the next moment, his hand yanked my ponytail, and I was pulled toward the car. I can still feel the shock of it. I told myself it was just one stormy night. But deep down, I knew better.

We married while I was still pregnant. The marriage was young but already cracking, its edges sharp. We fought over nothing, a look, a late return, and the silence that followed was heavier than the words.

About three years in, I enlisted in the Army, clinging to the idea that discipline and structure could give me the steady ground I'd never had. I learned to fold clothes with precision, to run until my lungs burned, to follow orders without hesitation. For a while, it felt like I was building a future I could trust, one I controlled.

But control slipped again the day I learned I was expecting our second child. The news brought both joy and dread, joy for the life I carried and dread for what it meant for my career. My voluntary discharge came with the same split in my chest: relief to go home and disappointment to leave what I'd worked so hard to prove I could do.

But suddenly, everything shifted.

Pregnancy didn't just bring morning sickness or swollen feet. I was dealing with some health issues. Would all the progress I'd made disappear the moment I couldn't wear a rucksack or stand in formation?

The decision to leave wasn't easy. It was filled with guilt and relief in equal parts. Under Chapter 8, pregnancy, voluntary discharge, I signed the papers and got ready to go home. My separation was honorable, and on paper, it looked simple. But emotionally, it was anything but.

I remember the last morning in uniform, the sensation of the fabric against my skin and the weight of the boots that had taken me through miles of discipline and pride. I stayed a little longer than necessary, soaking up how it all felt.

When I handed in my gear, defiance didn't fill my chest; it was grief. I was proud to have served. Proud to have come this far. But I was also walking away from a version of myself that had only just begun to believe she could handle hard things.

That day, I decided to leave the military and join the Inactive Army Reserve, a quiet goodbye, caught between relief and disappointment.

Because sometimes the hardest battles aren't the ones you fight on duty. They're the ones you fight within yourself, between who you were becoming and who life suddenly needs you to be.

Back home, I told myself I could make the marriage work. That was the lie I leaned on, believing that more effort, more patience, and more swallowing of my own needs might patch what was already splintered. Instead, the cracks widened. What I experienced next felt even more volatile: arguments that turned physical faster, words used as weapons, the kind of volatility that kept my nervous system braced.

My mother came for the birth of our second daughter. Her presence was a thin but vital line of safety between us. Just before she was born, his temper exploded again. He shoved me into chairs, his words slurred and venomous. My mother stepped between us, steady and fierce. "It takes a weak man to push a pregnant woman," she said. Even then, I stayed, clinging to the hope that two children might anchor us and that he could still become the man I once thought he was. But the storm never passed.

Two weeks after Linda was born, something happened I couldn't ignore. He took Kayla without telling me where he was going. Hours passed. I didn't know whether they were safe. That was the moment I finally went to court. With my mother's help, I regained custody of both girls. The weight of that protection order felt like both a shield and a goodbye. I packed what I could, gathered the girls, and walked out. For the first time, I believed I might keep us safe.

We left everything behind: the home, the marriage, the life I'd tried so hard to salvage.

At twenty-three, I wasn't just young; I was worn thin by the miles I'd traveled emotionally. I returned to Sarasota in 1997, not as the barefoot, wide-eyed girl who once rode her bike down 13th Street, but as a weary mother with a baby on my hip and another holding my hand. My body still ached from childbirth, but the heavier burden was invisible, the years of silent suffering, the mornings waking to the same hard truths.

I had no money, no plan, no backup, just two daughters who depended on me to keep standing when my own knees wanted to give out. My heart felt frayed, worn to threads so thin I barely recognized the woman in the mirror.

Sarasota hadn't changed much: sunlight spilling across the pavement like warm honey, palm trees swaying against an unbothered sky, the air faintly salted with heat. But I had changed. The streets I once knew looked different through the lens of survival. I didn't come back because I wanted to; I came back because there was nowhere else to go.

My grandfather's house, tucked in the same quiet corner of the city that held my childhood, became our reluctant haven. The moment I stepped inside, the past brushed against me: the scent of bacon on Sunday mornings, the creak of the hallway floorboard, the low hum of Paw Paw's voice from the kitchen. He had always been my calm in a world that felt dangerous. His hands, worn from work, had never once caused me harm. His presence was steady in a life that had been anything but.

Now, standing on Paw Paw's porch, I looked at the man who had once been my shelter. Alzheimer's had crept in like fog on a cold morning, slow, disorienting, impossible to push back. The man who used to hold my hand through nightmares now searched my face with eyes that didn't quite recognize me. He couldn't steady me anymore. My chest ached with the kind of heartbreak that has no tidy release. But I had nowhere else to go. This was still the safest place I knew.

There was no roadmap for rebuilding your life from the splinters of bad choices and grief. I stood in my grandfather's living room with swollen ankles, a stitched-up body, and the newborn's relentless cry echoing in my ears. The TV murmured softly; Paw Paw rocked slowly in his chair, unaware that I was unraveling. I had escaped, yes, but I'd also arrived in a place where survival was the only compass I had left.

Linda was only three weeks old, so small she seemed to disappear into the crook of his arm. He'd tickle her round belly, murmuring "coochy-coo" in the voice only grandfathers have. Even as Alzheimer's blurred his memory, he was still the Paw Paw I knew, the steady, gentle presence I needed most. I'd catch him watching her sleep, his face soft in a way that said he didn't need to remember everything to know she was his.

Kayla, three years old, was another story, wild and bright, bounding through the room with uncontainable energy. He loved her just as much, though her spark puzzled him. It made me laugh, even in that season of heaviness. Those moments, his quiet devotion to Linda and his bewildered smile at Kayla, reminded me that even when everything else was falling apart, love could still live in the small, ordinary gestures.

Somehow, I scraped together courage, piece by jagged piece, like gathering shards of a broken plate and trying to make them whole again. I stood under the shower, hot water pounding my shoulders, willing it to wash away the fear that clung like a second skin. In the mirror, a pale, tired woman stared back, eyes older than her years. "I whispered to her, 'You can do this. You must do this.'"

I painted my makeup like battle paint, each stroke meant to hide the exhaustion, the doubt. I slipped into the only decent outfit I had left, the one that, for a moment, made me feel like I might still belong in the world, and stepped out the door.

A baby carrier swung from one hand, my daughter's soft breaths warm against my wrist. In the other, I clutched a folder of crumpled résumés, their edges worn thin from being pulled out, handed over, and quietly set aside too many times.

I pounded the pavement, drifting from strip malls to greasy fast-food counters to dim temp agencies. Each waiting room buzzed under harsh fluorescent lights that stripped the warmth from the walls and the color from people's faces. I sat filling out forms beside men and women with that same faraway stare, the look of someone whose life had skidded off-script, quietly, desperately trying to write a new one.

I lost count of how many doors I walked through that month and how many polite smiles and "We'll call you" goodbyes I collected. Each rejection stung a little less, mostly because I couldn't afford to let it. My days blurred into a rhythm of survival, bottles, bills, job applications, repeat. But somewhere in that blur, something bigger was waiting. I didn't know it then, but I was walking straight toward the door that would change everything, the one that would lead me to a headset, to purpose, and eventually to myself.

# CHAPTER 2

## WHERE THE NOISE BEGINS

Inside the Sarasota County Administration Building, I moved down a hallway with mauve-painted walls; the color had faded to a dusty rose under the fluorescent lights. My footsteps clicked against stone floors, the sound bouncing ahead of me in the empty corridor. Near the exit, a corkboard sagged under the weight of years, layered with curling church announcements, sun-faded GED fliers, and job postings, so worn that their tear-off tabs hung like ragged teeth.

But one sign stopped me. It hung crooked, the edges curling, fluttering just enough under the air conditioning's hum to catch my attention. The black letters stood out against white paper, the kind of font that didn't waste time on decoration. Something about it felt different, as if it were meant for me.

Telecommunication Operators Wanted.

I froze mid-step. *Telecommunications?* The word tugged at something buried deep.

Army days at Fort Gordon came rushing back in fragments, PT at dawn, the ache in my calves as the sky turned pink. Formation in crisp lines, boots in perfect rows. Chow steaming in the mess hall, the scent of coffee and powdered eggs mingling in the air.

13

Then the vault-cold rooms, lit only by the eerie green glow of the green-screen terminals. Even the walls seemed to be listening.

I could almost hear the cadence of boots on pavement, feel the low hum of equipment under my fingertips, and remember the quiet weight of knowing every keystroke mattered. Back then, I hadn't realized I was learning more than a job. I was learning to focus under pressure, to catch the smallest details, and to keep going when it mattered most. Skills I'd need again, only next time the stakes might be even higher.

We moved information like lifeblood, encrypted, verified, precise, down to the last character. "Need-to-know" wasn't just a rule; it was the air we breathed. By the time I left, I could send a classified message with the same ease as signing my name. It wasn't glamorous, but it was a lifeline, and we kept it alive.

The memory dissolved, and I was back in the present, staring at a scrap of paper with a phone number on it. *Telecommunications.*

Not the Army, but close enough. Answer the phone. Take notes. Send the right help. Straightforward, at least that's what I told myself.

I slipped the number into my bag as if it were still a classified document. Old habits die hard. Maybe it wasn't combat, but it was another kind of mission, one where lives could hinge on whether I got it right.

Oh, I would learn.

What I walked into wasn't a job; it was an entire hidden ecosystem. Urgency pulsed, and the emotional residue of others' worst moments accumulated in the silence between calls. Behind those glowing screens lay high-stakes triage, psychological chess, and emotional minefields. No one wore body armor, yet the impact left its mark.

The hiring process was my first test of endurance. On paper, it was a three-month process. In my anxious chest, it felt like a year had passed.

The first step was *an observation*. It sounded harmless enough until I sat beside a 911 operator at a live console.

I was actually sitting next to a *real* 911 operator, and I was stoked.

Her headset hugged her jaw, the coiled cord trailing into the console like a lifeline. Her fingers moved nonstop, tapping keys, flipping screens, and answering calls almost before the first ring had finished. The room buzzed with voices and radio chatter, a low undercurrent of urgency that felt both foreign and familiar, like stepping into the control room of chaos itself.

I slipped on my own headset, heart pounding, and listened in. The calls came fast, bursts of panic, confusion, and sudden quiet. She spoke with practiced calm, her tone steady no matter what poured through the line. I remember thinking: *How does she do that? How can someone sound so still when everything on the other end is falling apart?*

In that moment, something clicked. I didn't fully understand it yet, but I knew I wanted to be that calm in the storm.

"How long have you been doing this?" I asked, trying not to stare at the speed of her hands.

"About three years," she said without looking away from the screen. "Long days. No such thing as a slow one, really."

"Do you ever… get used to it?" My voice came out quieter than I'd intended.

She smirked faintly, still typing. "You learn to get used to it. It doesn't mean it gets easier. It means you stop noticing how much you're holding."

I glanced at her as she flipped through screens. "How do you know which one to focus on?"

Her fingers danced over the keyboard. "Depends on what's

screaming the loudest, callers, radio, alarms. You learn to listen with more than your ears."

The phone lit up again. She answered without missing a beat. "911, what's the location of the emergency?" Her tone shifted instantly, calm and steady, a voice you could hold onto in the dark.

She hung up moments later and kept typing.

"Do you get calls like that all the time on 911?" I asked.

"Oh, a noise complaint. Yes, they don't know the difference. Their neighbor says someone's drumming in the garage. I'll send a unit, but we've got bigger fires right now."

I nodded, unsure what counted as a "big fire" in her world. "Do you ever think about what happens after you hang up?"

Her jaw tightened slightly. "Sometimes. Most of the time, you can't. You move on to the next call."

The calls kept coming, one after another, layered over the low murmur of radio traffic and the chatter of other operators. The room felt alive, as if every console were a beating heart in the same body. Watching it in motion made me want to prove I could belong here and keep up with the rhythm.

That opportunity came sooner than I expected. No sooner had the observation ended than it was time for the Oral Board, an interview conducted by a full panel in the coming days.

The name sounded harmless enough until they led me into a room where three uniformed professionals sat in a neat row behind a long table. The air felt cooler in there, yet heavier, as if it had been waiting for me.

Their eyes tracked me as range instructors watched recruits on the firing line, quiet and assessing, and I interpreted that as them deciding whether I belonged. I'd been here before, in a way. Different room, different uniforms, but the same unspoken challenge: *Show us who you are. Show us if you belong.*

I was already sweating when I sat down, my palms glued to the smooth chair arms, my pulse thumping in my ears like a warning drum. Somewhere deep in my gut, I knew this wasn't going to be a job you "ease into." This was a locked gate, and the people in front of me held the only keys.

They didn't waste time.

"This is a 24/7 job, weekends, holidays, hurricanes, and every family event you'll ever miss," one of them said, his voice steady yet unyielding. "How do you plan to manage that schedule?"

Another leaned forward. "Tell us about yourself."

A third followed with, "Give an example of a time you had to multitask under pressure."

Multitask? At that moment, I couldn't even remember my own name. My carefully rehearsed answers scattered like startled pigeons, leaving only static in my head, the kind you hear on a radio between stations.

I opened my mouth, and something came out. To this day, I couldn't tell you what it was. I remember the heat creeping up my neck, the tremble in my hands, and the unshakable certainty that I was failing spectacularly, live and in person.

When it was over, I stepped into the hallway as the door thudded shut behind me. It sounded final, like a gavel. Well, I thought, at least I didn't burst into flames. They're never going to call me back.

Years later, I'd be on the other side of that same table, the one that once felt like a firing squad. By then, I was more seasoned, a little scarred, but wiser. I could spot the wide-eyed terror instantly, the silent plea of please don't let me screw this up etched across their faces.

I'd smile, even as I asked those same pointed questions. I'd root for them quietly, willing their voices to steady, because I remembered exactly what it felt like to sit in that chair, trying not to sweat through my shirt while praying I didn't trip over my own words. I remembered, and I knew.

If the Oral Board felt like a firing squad, the Prefex test, long before CritiCall existed, felt like an elaborate prank dreamed up by a sadistic game show host. The machine looked like a prop stolen from an old Star Trek set, with knobs to twist, sliders to yank, and blinking lights that mocked you with no mercy. Every sequence had to be perfect, every movement exact, while your brain scrambled to keep pace.

I thought I had it under control. My hands moved almost on autopilot, chasing the lights across the console, when suddenly the rotary phone bolted to the side shrieked to life. I grabbed the receiver, expecting a straightforward question. Instead, a garbled, static-choked scream ripped through the earpiece. A woman's voice, frantic and broken, spitting words like shrapnel. My task? Transcribe every single word.

Panic surged. My pen stuttered. All I could hear was the pounding of my own heartbeat, drowning out her words. For a split second, I froze, in the nightmare moment every dispatcher dreads.

When it was over, I sat there blinking, my heart pounding, my notes a tangle of half-legible scrawl. I walked out convinced I'd just flunked it.

And yet… somehow, I passed.

After the four-hour observation, the Oral Board firing squad, and the Prefex Test from another galaxy, I proceeded to the background check.

Easy peasy, I thought.

I'd just been poked, prodded, and practically fingerprinted down to my DNA by the Army for a Top-Secret clearance. Compared to that, this felt like nothing at all.

But the thing about "easy" is that it often comes with fine print. I hadn't yet realized that this wasn't just about passing a background check; it was about stepping into a world where every move, every word, and every mistake could follow you for years.

It took two long months, two months of having my life picked apart as if they were prepping for a documentary. They wanted everything: every address I'd ever lived at, every job I'd ever held, every acquaintance I'd so much as waved to in a grocery store parking lot. They asked for my financial history, my criminal record (mercifully squeaky clean), and probably would've taken an inventory of my glove compartment if I'd offered.

What I didn't understand then was the extent to which this job demanded discretion, professionally, ethically, and emotionally. They weren't just hiring someone to answer phones; they were preparing to hand me the keys to the county's most sensitive information: law enforcement databases, dispatch systems, and the unfiltered details of people's most vulnerable moments. They needed to know I was solid, that I wouldn't crack under pressure, that I could keep my mouth shut when it mattered, and most of all, that I could stand steady when the worst of humanity came pouring through a phone line.

Eventually, the call came. I'd made it.

Just like that, I wasn't the woman scanning corkboards and clutching grocery bags, wondering whether I'd ever matter again. I was a trainee, soon to be wearing a headset that would plug me straight into the best and worst of humanity.

The first step? A trip to the quartermaster.

It was a plain, windowless room that smelled faintly of starch, dust, and the metallic tang of filing cabinets that had been there since the '70s. Shelves lined the walls, stacked with bins labeled by badge number, each holding the armor we'd wear into emotional combat.

When the staff member called my name, I stepped forward, trying to summon the confidence I didn't yet feel. She handed me a stack of green polyester pants stiff enough to stand on their own, crisp white button-up shirts, a shiny badge, a metal nameplate etched with my name in bold black letters, and a standard-issue utility belt.

I held it all as if it were sacred. I hadn't expected uniforms, but the moment I saw my name staring back at me from that brushed metal, something shifted. This wasn't a maybe anymore. This was real. Tangible. It had weight.

The annual pay was $18,000. On paper, it was nothing to brag about. But to me, it was oxygen. It covered groceries, gas, baby wipes, electricity, and the first rung on a ladder out of the dark. A lifeline, disguised as a job.

But I didn't walk into that center as a blank slate. I came in hauling a freight train of unspoken pain, decades of childhood trauma, the sting of domestic violence, the wreckage of a marriage, and a silence so well-rehearsed it had fused into my DNA. I didn't talk about it. I couldn't. There wasn't room. Two little girls were counting on me to get this right.

Failure wasn't just unacceptable.

It was unthinkable.

In February 1998, 911 Operator Training began in the old Terrace Building downtown, a faded relic perched at the corner of Washington and Ringling. The third floor doubled as our emergency backup center and looked the part. The Mezzanine floor was known to be haunted at night. The carpet was worn thin along the paths we all walked, chairs groaned when you sat in them, and the technology looked like it had been rescued from a Cold War Museum, dusty, temperamental, but stubbornly functional.

There were five or six of us in the class, a mixed group of hopefuls, each carrying our private reasons for being there. Some were seeking a career shift, others stability, but we all shared the same hunger: to prove we could handle this.

In those early days, walking into the dispatch center felt a lot like transferring to a new high school halfway through the year; everyone already had their circle, their shorthand, their rhythm. I was the quiet one, careful not to trip over my own feet, listening more than I spoke. Still, there was comfort in numbers, and I found my first thread of connection in Kim.

We met at the academy, two brand-new recruits, both terrified, both pretending not to be. Kim had a quick wit that could cut through tension with a single one-liner. I admired that about her. She made the air in the room feel a little lighter, as if maybe we weren't about to be crushed under the weight of everything we were learning. I was quieter. More serious. More unsure.

One afternoon, during a simulation, the instructor barked orders so fast that my brain felt scrambled. My fingers froze over the keyboard, panic bubbling just below the surface. The whole room went silent as everyone watched me stall. Then Kim leaned back in her chair, smirked, and said, loud enough for everyone to hear:

"Well, if dispatch doesn't work out, at least Kris has a promising career as a deer in headlights."

The room erupted in laughter, the kind that broke tension rather than bruised it. Even the instructor cracked a grin. My cheeks burned, but the knot in my chest loosened. I laughed too, because she wasn't mocking me. She was saving me. With one joke, Kim shifted the moment from humiliating to human.

Kim and I were close in age, but our lives couldn't have been more different. She joined the others for drinks after class, unwinding with laughter and beer. I went home to babies, bills, and the constant weight of responsibility. But in the academy, we found our rhythm, sharing glances during simulations, sitting side by side during drills, and whispering in the hallway when nerves got the better of us. Shared fear. Shared hope. We were in it together, and that made it survivable.

We started with the basics: ten-codes, signals, call types, and documentation procedures. The dispatcher's alphabet and grammar. Flashcards became my constant companion. I tucked them into my diaper bag, stuck them to the refrigerator, and stacked them on the kitchen counter. I flipped through them while stirring macaroni and cheese, while rocking my baby to sleep, and while whispering acronyms into the bathroom mirror at 2 a.m. Sleep wasn't an option. Stopping wasn't an option. I couldn't afford to let anything slip.

What we were learning wasn't just about memorizing codes; it was about stepping into a whole new way of thinking. Dispatch had its own language, a shorthand in which every number and every word carried weight. A wrong code or a missed address wasn't just a mistake; it could cost someone time, and that could lead to something even deadlier.

Even though I'd grown up in Sarasota, I was learning the city all over again, not as the place where I'd played tag in the streets or watched fireworks over the bay, but as a tactical map. Streets I'd once known by sight now had to be known by instinct. Nostalgia didn't help. You had to know the city by muscle, not memory.

We broke Sarasota into zones, color-coded with highlighters in thick binders that smelled of dry-erase markers and anxiety. Zone 1 was near the airport. Zone 2, next to it, was off University Boulevard. Each area had its own rhythm, its own signature chaos.

We didn't just memorize locations; we studied them like soldiers researching terrain. Grid books became our bibles. Every square was a potential crisis. Every page could mean the difference between saving someone... or losing precious seconds we could never get back.

We sat at our desks with map books fanned open like tactical overlays, tracing the grid lines with our fingertips. "Bee Ridge and Tuttle" wasn't just an intersection anymore; it was a nexus of response times, jurisdictional quirks, and caller confusion. I started hearing street names in my sleep, the syllables looping through my dreams.

We were trained to visualize routes in real time, as if we were in the passenger seat of the responding unit: Northbound. Eastbound. Where's the shortest access point to Zone 2? Who's the closest unit in the zone? You had to see it in your head before you could say it out loud.

Verification wasn't optional; it was survival. Cross streets. Landmarks. Apartment numbers tucked behind unlit driveways. A call from "Walmart" meant nothing until you pinpointed which one, off Cattlemen or the one on 41? If you guessed, you failed. If you hesitated, help arrived too late. There was no wiggle room. No "close enough." Accuracy wasn't a goal; it was the law of the land. Lives were measured in feet and seconds. You had to be right. The first time. Every time.

And it wasn't just logistics; it was responsibility, a weight in my chest. Every time I hit send on a location, I knew what I was putting into motion. If I got it wrong, someone's life could hang in the balance. It wasn't glamorous work. It was pressure that tightened your shoulders and made you second-guess yourself in the early days. But after enough reps, the hesitation burned away. You got faster. Sharper. More automatic.

That's how you survived dispatch: not by remembering your hometown, but by rebuilding it, street by street, call by call, until the city lived in your bones like coordinates etched in code.

Then came the day I was assigned a training officer, the day you "hit the floor" for real calls. The beginning. The moment they test your grit.

My stomach was a fistful of knots. My training officer didn't exactly greet me warmly, more of a brisk, businesslike nod. But then again, I wasn't exactly Miss Sunshine in first meetings either. I was quiet, guarded, already bracing for whatever was coming.

"Sit here. Plug in here. Listen to me," she said. So I did.

We sat at C13, a non-emergency call-taking position. Far enough from the main radio channels to be out of the fire, yet close enough to feel the heartbeat of the room. We sat shoulder to shoulder, connected to the console by a Y-cord; her headset was live, mine just a dead plastic device, muted against my head. Ready to listen.

She took the first few calls, her voice a masterclass in calm efficiency. Steady. Quick. No wasted words, no wasted movement. Watching her was like watching a surgeon at work, precise, practiced, utterly unshaken.

I tried to memorize everything: the way her fingers danced across the keyboard, how she layered listening with typing, and the subtle lift in her tone when she needed information fast.

Then she turned to me.

"Okay," she said. "You're up next."

"Who, me? Do I have to? I spoke

"Yes. It's time to start taking your calls," she answered

The room seemed to shift. The air grew heavier. My throat tightened until I could feel my pulse in it. Every nerve in my body screamed, Run!

Every ounce of second-guessing I'd ever carried seemed to rush through me at once. It was as if my entire life had been a rehearsal for hesitation. From the time I was a child, I'd learned the safest place was inside myself, quiet, small, unseen. I'd mastered silence in trailer parks and courtrooms, in the shadow of my father's control and amid the storms of my first marriage. I could disappear in plain sight, make myself untouchable by not speaking at all.

But this wasn't the time to disappear. Not here. Not with a headset in my hand and a line about to open. This was supposed to be the moment to find my voice, to plant it firmly and trust it could hold.

I wasn't there yet.

Confidence didn't live in me then; it hovered just out of reach, like something other people had. I felt small in that chair, my back stiff, my palms damp against the console. Weak. Under-skilled. Uncertain about everything, from my typing speed to whether my voice would even sound right over the line.

The Army had taught me discipline, how to stand straight, follow orders, and push through exhaustion. But it hadn't taught me to believe in myself.

Surviving domestic violence had taught me grit and how to keep moving when everything in me wanted to shut down. But it hadn't taught me how to speak without fear.

Endurance was my only real skill at the time. I could take the hit, hold my breath, and wait for the storm to pass by.

What I didn't see yet was that endurance would get me through the door, but it wouldn't keep me standing once I was inside. For that, I'd have to learn something new.

But dispatch wasn't a place to hold your breath. The storm didn't pass here; it just kept coming, call after call after call. And in that moment, with my training officer watching and the next ring hanging in the air like a loaded question, I knew I had to step into it, whether I was ready or not.

So, I reached for the headset. Adjusted the mic. Hit the Ready button.

And took my first breath as a voice on the line said, "Dispatch Center, this line is recorded. This is Kris. How may I help you?"

My voice trembled, barely above a whisper. But it was mine. And it was the beginning of everything. That one sentence, my scripted introduction, became more than words I was required to say. It became my new identity. I repeated it dozens of times a shift until it no longer felt foreign, until it wrapped around me like armor, until it became the voice, a lifeline for someone else, even on the days I wasn't sure I had one for myself.

The calls came in fast. Relentless. Like waves pounding the shore, one after another, with barely a breath between them.

A neighbor complaining about a dog barking since sunrise.

A man, furious that his mailbox had been pried open, his voice shaking with indignation.

A fender bender in a Publix parking lot that escalated into two grown men screaming threats over a dented bumper.

Noise complaints. Stolen mail. Domestic violence. Car crashes. People angry about the noise. People terrified by shadows. People bleeding, screaming, breaking, reaching for help.

The entire county poured itself into my headset, its fears, its fury, its quiet despair, and I became the funnel. Their voices came in tangled, raw knots, and I had to shape them into something clear, something dispatchable.

I had to turn chaos into code.

Codes into units dispatched.

Units into officers on scene.

And into the only words most callers needed to hear: Help is on the way.

During training, we began with the "safe" tasks, such as non-emergency calls, noise complaints, lost wallets, and neighbors arguing over whose turn it was to mow the strip of grass between their driveways. It wasn't that emergencies never slipped onto those lines; they did, and sometimes they were wild. But non-emergency calls were where I learned the ropes, how to work the system, ask the right questions, and keep my tone even. It was training with a net.

Just when I thought I'd found my balance, they cut the net.

Now I would train on the 911 lines, a world utterly different from the one I'd just gotten used to. Wilder. Faster. As forgiving as a cat in a bathtub. Calls didn't arrive in the polite, evenly spaced intervals of the non-emergency lines. They came in hot, stacked on top of each other, without warning, slamming into you like a freight train you never saw coming.

That's not to say every 911 call was chaotic. Some were misdials, and others were from people who should've used the non-emergency line. But when that call hit your headset, the sharp, urgent chime that meant someone was calling 911, you braced yourself. Because more often than not, it meant a real emergency was about to spill through your earpiece, and you had to be ready before the first word left their mouth.

The tone in my ear was my warning shot, sharp, insistent, impossible to ignore. Every time I heard it, my heart jumped into my throat. I'd brace myself, a tight breath catching in my chest, fingers hovering over the keyboard. My headset pressed snug against my ear, like a lifeline, as if holding it closer might somehow make me smarter, faster... or at least sound like I knew what I was doing.

On that side of the console, there was no easing in. The moment the line opened, you were smack in the middle of someone's worst day, no warm-up, no stretching, no "let's just run through this slowly." Whatever came next, you had to meet it head-on, preferably without sounding as panicked as they were.

Sometimes the caller would speak calmly, almost unnervingly so, their voice steady as they described someone bleeding on the floor or a stranger trying to break down the door. Unlike the Prefex test, they weren't making it up, though in that moment I half-expected someone to yell "Gotcha!" just to see if I'd flinch.

Other times, the calls were pure chaos. I'd pick up and be met with screaming so loud the line crackled and distorted, as if someone had set their phone down in the middle of a heavy metal concert. My instinct was to match their volume; if they yelled, I yelled, so there I was, practically shouting into my headset on the dispatch floor.

"MA'AM, MA'AM" ……" MA'AM, MA'AM, I NEED TO GET THE ADDRESS!"

The room would go quiet, and I'd lean forward, straining to separate words from raw panic, silently begging them to pause for one tiny breath so I could figure out what the hell was happening.

After one boisterous call, my training officer swiveled toward me, a smirk tugging at the corner of her mouth.

"If you lower your voice," she said, "they'll have to lower theirs to hear you. It works more often than you'd think."

I nodded as if I'd just been handed the secret to life. "Okay," I told her. "I'll try it next time."

It took me quite a while to work that trick into my routine, but she was right; it did work.

This was 1998, just before cell phones took over. Back then, almost every call came from a landline, a home, a business, or a payphone, and that meant one gift in the chaos: the address popped up on my screen automatically, glowing like a beacon in the storm. Everything else, though, was guesswork.

My mind would race through the checklist, listening, typing, probing, reassuring, and routing, all at once. I didn't have the muscle memory yet. In some cases, I'd remember to calm the caller but forget half the details, like the time a man reported a burglary in progress and I soothed him for three whole minutes before realizing I'd never asked for the suspect's description. At other times, I'd be so focused on entering the information into CAD that I'd let the caller spiral out of control, like the woman reporting a car crash who went from frantic to near-hyperventilating while I was still deciding which drop-down field to select. My hands and brain hadn't learned to dance together yet.

That's where my training officer came in. Sitting beside me, plugged into the Y-cord, she could hear everything: the caller's voice, my voice, every keystroke. She'd nudge me if I froze, like during a domestic disturbance call when I forgot to ask whether the suspect was still on scene. She'd whisper a question in my ear if I missed something important, like "Did you get the direction of travel?" when a robbery suspect fled. Sometimes she'd point to the screen, tapping the notes section where I'd overlooked a clue in the caller's tone, such as hesitation that hinted they might know their "intruder" personally, or a sudden drop in volume that meant the danger was getting closer.

Every call was a jolt, both electrical and emotional. A woman hiding in her closet. A man clutching his chest. A child whispering that Daddy had a gun. If it were a medical emergency, I'd transfer them to EMS for life-saving instructions. If it were law enforcement, I'd stay with them. My job was to be the calm in the storm, keep them talking, and gather every detail until help arrived.

One night, I took my first prowler call, a Signal 27.

The address popped up instantly. That part was easy. The rest? Not so much.

"911, what's the location of the emergency?"

"There's... there's someone in my yard," the woman said, her voice trembling. "I can see him through the blinds... he's just standing there."

"What is your address, ma'am?"

"I'm at a house on Beneva

I verified the address, and then I typed Signal 27 – prowler, my fingers tripping over the keys. "Ma'am, stay on the line with me. Where exactly in your yard is he?"

"In the back... near the shed. Oh my God, he's moving."

I glanced at my training officer, who motioned for me to keep her talking. "Is he carrying anything? What's he wearing?"

"A dark hoodie... jeans... I think he's looking at the house." She stopped. I heard her breath quicken.

"Um..Okay, I need you to stay calm. Doors locked?"

"Yes."

"Lights on?"

"I don't want him to see me!"

I hesitated. My training officer tapped the desk. "Keep her focused."

"That's okay, just stay low. Do you have a dog?

She whispered, "No. Just me."

While I spoke, my other hand was sending the call up, dispatching units with the correct codes and signals to get the dispatcher's attention. I could hear the radio behind me crackle as deputies called out en route.

"He's walking toward the side gate," she whispered.

I kept my voice steady even as my pulse hammered. "Stay on the line with me. Deputies are on their way. I'll tell you the second they arrive."

Two minutes later, though it felt like twenty, I heard the dispatcher acknowledge the units on the other side of the room say, "Copy, 3212

"They're there now," I told her.

When she hung up, I leaned back, my shoulders aching from how tightly I'd been holding them. My training officer gave me a brief nod. "Nice job," she said.

That's when I realized the pounding in my chest wasn't just adrenaline from the call. It was the same fight-or-flight I'd carried since childhood. The quick scans, the measured breathing, the way I kept my voice calm while my insides raced. Surviving had taught me those skills long before I ever wore a headset. That night, I learned to use them for someone else's survival, too.

During training, I also learned quickly that not every 911 call was an emergency.

One evening, the line lit up, and I answered, with my training officer plugged in beside me.

"911, what's the location of your emergency?" I asked, trying to keep my tone steady.

A man said, with complete seriousness, "Yeah, I need an officer because my neighbor's cat keeps sitting on my car. I just washed it, and this is the third time today."

I hesitated for just a second before answering, but my trainer gave me a slight nod to continue.

"Sir, that's not something for 911," I explained carefully. "If you'd like, I can give you our non-emergency number so you can report it there."

He sighed like I'd just dismissed the crime of the century but eventually agreed to take the number.

A few shifts later, I picked up another call that began with a whisper. My pulse jumped.

"There's a man outside my house," the woman said.

I kept my voice calm. "Can you describe him?"

"He's wearing brown. He's... uh... pushing a cart."

"Is he armed?" I asked, bracing myself.

"No... he's selling ice cream."

I glanced at my trainer, and she quietly leaned over. "Not every whisper means danger," she said.

Moments like that stuck with me. They taught me that part of dispatch wasn't just about emergencies; it was about sorting the real from the imagined and the urgent from the inconvenient, while maintaining a steady voice through it all.

I would be so proud of myself when I nailed calls, but at other times I stumbled, chasing details as they outran me. But that was the point of training, to show you what panic sounded like and teach you how to stay grounded anyway. Those first 911 calls didn't make me fearless. They didn't make me confident. It was something in between, like stepping into fire and realizing you could stand the heat.

Breaks were scheduled every few hours; take them when you can. To get away from the stress of the room, training, and calls.

While we took those much-needed breaks, went to the bathroom, the break room, and the vending machine to grab an unhealthy snack (a Snickers Bar or something that would try to recharge your soul), it never seemed long enough. On paper, we were allotted a fifteen-minute pause every couple of hours, a generous slice of time, apparently, to breathe, regroup, maybe even remember what it felt like to be human. But what exactly can fifteen minutes do after two straight hours of holding someone else's worst moment in your chest? It wasn't recovery time. It was just long enough to pretend we weren't coming apart at the seams.

Lunch and dinner weren't sacred pauses, either. They were stolen moments at our consoles, food more often cold than hot, half-chewed between calls. Sometimes the first bite didn't even make it past your teeth before the headset chimed. That soft tone in your ear was like the starting gun at an Olympic sprint, except the race was to keep someone alive, and you were running it with a mouthful of chicken nuggets.

The idea of sitting in a breakroom with your feet up and a warm meal was pure fiction. We didn't have the staffing for luxuries like that. You grabbed what you could, when you could. Dinner was whatever fit in a to-go box and could survive being ignored for an hour, a slice of pizza balanced on a napkin beside the CAD terminal. A plastic fork abandoned midair over lukewarm pasta when the next emergency cut through the hum of the room. If you were lucky, you'd remember where you left the fork before the noodles glued themselves into one tragic carb brick.

The soundtrack never stopped, radios hissing, phones ringing, voices volleying across the floor. The glow of blinking console lights was your candlelight dinner, ambiance, and all. Some nights, we traded jokes between bites, trying to make the air light enough to breathe. Other nights, we just chewed in silence, the lump in our throats bigger than the food we were forcing down.

You learned to digest stress along with your dinner. To take a breath between bites and emergencies. To pick up the next call while your food went cold because the next voice was already there. And ready or not, you had to answer.

Back then, I smoked. That was my release.

During what could be called a break, I would head to the far end of the admin building, a spot rarely visited except by those seeking a brief escape. The sounds of keyboard typing and dispatch radio chatter faded into a distant hum of traffic noise, soft enough to resemble the ocean when you listened closely. If you listened hard and long enough, you could hear Sarasota Bay; we were only a few blocks away. Streetlights cast pale yellow halos onto the pavement, creating an atmosphere that felt heavier and more peaceful.

I'd fish a cigarette from the crumpled pack in my pocket, light it with hands still stressed from the last call and drag in the smoke like it was oxygen. The first inhale always hit the hardest, sharp and bitter, the burn racing down my throat. I'd hold it in for a beat, pretending it might sear away the residue of panic still clinging to my ribs, then exhale slowly, watching the smoke curl and twist before the night swallowed it whole.

Somewhere in my head, I convinced myself I could exhale the stress, that if I blew the smoke out hard enough, it might carry away the mistake from the last call, the weight of training, the grind of the hours. I told myself the metallic taste of fear in my mouth could be masked by nicotine. It was a lie, but it worked just enough to get me back upstairs.

A few deep breaths, a final flick of ash, and the glowing ember was gone, stubbed out and left in the little concrete ashtray by the door. The elevator ride back up was always too short. Then it was back through the buzzing keycard doors, into the hum of fluorescent lights and the cold glow of computer screens. Back to my console. Back into the storm.

My world had narrowed to a single mission: Get it right.

Learn the layout. Memorize the zones. Verify the address every time. Code the call accurately. Keep the caller calm enough to get the details we need. Speak clearly. Type faster. Think three steps ahead. Don't miss a beat.

The comm center was laid out like a battlefield, organized chaos carved into precise sections. Call takers lined one side, fire dispatchers worked the back, PD and SO dispatch flanked the edges, and the supervisor sat in the center like a hawk, scanning the whole room, ready to swoop down the second something went sideways.

It was noisy in a way that was both controlled and unnerving, a constant hum of overlapping voices, the hiss of static from open mics, the sharp ping of incoming calls, the ring of the overflow bell, and the clatter of keyboards tapping like Morse code. Yet in that dimly lit room, you learned to hear what mattered.

At that stage, I was only learning call-taking, my lane, my training ground. Even that felt monumental. My job was to keep my focus on the voice in my ear while keeping one part of my brain tuned to the room around me. That was the unspoken skill: the art of divided attention.

Sometimes, two of us would pick up calls about the same incident, one from the victim and the other from a neighbor or witness. If we were sharp, we could merge the calls before two separate units were dispatched to the same incident. That required finesse, focus, and a sixth sense for the rhythm of the room.

Situational Awareness and multitasking weren't things you learned from a PowerPoint slide. They were forged in the sweat of real-time problem-solving, balancing a panicked voice in one ear while catching the quiet code words murmured by a dispatcher across the room in the other. You learned to stretch your awareness like elastic without snapping.

I poured everything I had into that headset, my anxiety, my determination, and my need to prove I could finally be good at something that mattered. There were no shortcuts. No cheat sheets. Only long nights, raw nerves, and a stack of index cards covered in my scribbled ten-codes and street names.

And then, one day, after three months of rotating shifts, changing training officers, and living with a constant voice in my ear, my training officer looked at me across the console and said, "You are good to be on your own."

I was being released from training.

It felt like someone had unclipped my harness at the edge of a cliff and whispered, *Fly*. (And for the record, I'm terrified of heights.) My heart thudded so hard I could hear it in my ears. I thought about the journey that brought me here, the tears, the frustrations, the moments when my attitude nearly got the best of me, and yet I'd made it. This was the moment. No more "just listening." No more safety net beside me, ready to catch me if I froze. It was just me now, me, my headset, my console, and an entire county waiting for me to answer.

The chair felt different beneath me, as if it knew the training wheels were gone. The console's lights seemed sharper, the room louder, every sound suddenly magnified. The distant hiss of radio static. The sharp ping of an incoming line. The faint rustle of papers from three consoles away. My fingers hovered over the keyboard, already tight with anticipation.

And then the thought settled in, cold and certain: the next voice could belong to anyone.

A mother screaming because her child wasn't breathing.

A teenager whispering through a locked bedroom door, praying he wouldn't find her.

A man whose voice would fade out completely before help could get there.

That was my job now. No second headset. No second chance.

Just me.

And the next call.

I didn't know it yet, but my real education was about to begin. Training had been the rehearsal. Now came the show, and there was no script.

# CHAPTER 3

## THE SIGNAL INSIDE THE NOISE

When a high-priority call came in, it consumed you whole. There was no preparation, no warning bell that said, 'Get ready, this one's going to change everything.' No script could capture the way panic sounds when it's strangling someone's voice. No second chance if you missed the thing they didn't know how to say. You had to think three steps ahead while staying rooted in the present. One second of hesitation could cost everything.

Bam, it was in your ear, in all its screaming glory. And you had to react. Now.

Not later, not after you processed, not after you caught your breath.

Now. And you had to know what to do. Now.

For Priority 0 or 1 calls, the standard was gospel: get it up in 30 seconds or less. Verify the address. Get the cross street. Confirm the phone number. Code it. Send it to dispatch. Fast. Clean. Precise. Because seconds weren't just seconds; they were outcomes.

In those first months, every time that tone hit my ear, I felt that truth. I felt the pressure to assess the call within seconds and get it to dispatch with the right information quickly. That's a lot to carry.

And then there was my first bank robbery, with the same split-second precision I'd learned in the Army, only here the battlefield was a blinking cursor and a stranger's voice.

Evening shift. Around 5:00 p.m., as Sarasota's daytime crowd merged into rush hour and the shadows lengthened across Bee Ridge like warning signs, the center flowed with its usual rhythm, phones chiming, radios crackling, and the soft murmur of overlapping updates, when the tone suddenly sounded.

I straightened instantly, fingers hovering over the keyboard.

"911, what is the location of your emergency?"

Her voice came through calm, but too calm, the kind of calm that's more about control than composure. Rushed. Clipped and flattened by shock.

"This is a local bank. We were just robbed at gunpoint."

The words lit up every nerve ending in my body.

"What's the address?" I asked, already seeing the ANI/ALI information scrolling down my screen.

"An address on Bee Ridge Road."

"What's the nearest cross street?"

She provided it to me quickly, as I was flipping through my grid book before she finished. Back then, we didn't trust technology alone; you verified in print, eyes scanning for the correct zone, page edges softened by years of sweaty fingers. Bee Ridge. Got it.

I coded it fast: Signal 41 for robbery. Then added Signal 0, gun involved. No hesitation. I verified the callback number. Fingers flying, I typed the first comments: Signal 41 Signal 0 GUN (Robbery at gunpoint. Suspect armed).

Send. Marked Priority 0.

Elapsed time: 25 seconds.

Now the details.

36

"Do you know what he looked like?"

"White male. He had a mask on. I think he had on a dark shirt and jeans."

Line by line, it went into the call: WM, MASK, LSW DRK SHRT, JNS. (White Male, Mask, Last Seen Wearing, dark shirt and jeans)

"What did he leave in?"

"A blue sedan. He left eastbound on Bee Ridge."

LSD BLU SEDAN, LSH EB Bee Ridge. (Last Seen Driving Blue Sedan, Last Seen Heading Eastbound on Bee Ridge)

No dye pack. No injuries. The call moved like lightning, every word sharp, every second heavy. My hands worked almost faster than my brain could process, muscle memory kicking in before thought. My voice stayed steady, but my heart pounded so hard I could feel it in my jaw.

Less than two minutes later, the call was over. The air in my headset is still warm against my ear, and my fingertips tingle from the adrenaline.

A robbery. A gun. A fleeing suspect. And I was the one who answered.

It was the same kind of rapid, precise thinking I'd learned in the Army, only here the battlefield was a blinking cursor and a line full of voices, no time to think. No pause. No slow breath. The next tone was already stabbing through my headset, pulling me into another call before the weight of the first could even settle.

While I was still finding my place, I started to understand the environment, noticing the constant glow of lines and the personalities that filled the space between. Some coworkers were open and approachable, engaging in conversations as if it were natural. During the space between calls, we shared stories about recent calls, how they ended, near-misses, and those that went completely off the rails. This was my way of learning the skills of the job, seeing how others handled their calls, taking notes to gain an advantage, and passing the time during long hours tethered to a station. We exchanged tips on urgent calls, shared glimpses of family life, and discussed kids, vacations, and weekend plans.

Regarding the family section, I participated superficially. I kept my true stories hidden, only nodding, smiling, and sharing a few safe details without fully opening up. My childhood was marked by abuse, and I wasn't prepared to confront or discuss it. I only began to reveal my past through therapy and ultimately while writing this book.

So inside dispatch, I wore a mask. People around me saw the closed-off edges, the standoffishness, the unapproachable air. What they didn't see was that I wasn't protecting them from me. I was protecting myself from them. Trust was currency, and mine was buried in a vault no one had the combination to. And when you walk into a room full of Type-A personalities, it's tough. Really tough.

I didn't know how to communicate with people who weren't broken. From the very beginning, I was built differently. I didn't have a normal childhood, and it showed. The ease with which my coworkers interacted, the way they slipped into conversation, shared stories, and laughed freely, felt foreign to me. That Type A personality so many dispatchers carried like armor? I wasn't born with it. I had to learn it piece by piece, just as I had learned the layout of the consoles.

Between calls, we'd dissect the work, discussing how to set up a call in CAD and how to ensure units had what they needed before they requested it. Sometimes we touched on the heavier stuff, the calls that sat like stones in your chest. There was an unspoken understanding that you didn't have to explain why a certain voice stuck with you; everyone in the room had their own.

But not everyone met you with softness. Some veterans wouldn't bother to learn your name until you'd survived a whole year on the floor. They called it a rite of passage. I called it a cold shoulder. I remember the sting of invisibility, the quick glance at my screen, the silent printout of my mistakes, dropped on the supervisor's desk without a word to me, as if I hadn't yet earned the right to be spoken to.

And then... There were the ones who surprised me. Beneath their hardened shells, a few took the time to teach. I remember one veteran, Rick, waving me over during a rare lull. "You put comments on the screen in the wrong order," he told me. "When an officer is driving to the scene, they need the suspect description first, not what the suspect stole. That comes later. Give them what they need to find the threat." It was a small lesson, but one that stuck. In this job, order wasn't just about neatness; it was about survival.

It clicked instantly. The dispatcher wasn't trying to embarrass me; he was trying to keep people alive. That's when I realized: every call, every critique, every correction was tied to something much bigger than me.

Still, there were nights when the stress boiled over. During hot calls, the room would vibrate with urgency, dispatchers yelling across consoles, radio traffic colliding with phone rings. Then suddenly: "C17!" they'd shout, never my name. "WHAT IS THE SUSPECT WEARING?" in the nastiest way ever. (Or at least that's how my broken brain heard it.) And there I'd be, on the phone with the most difficult caller in Florida, trying to pull answers from someone more interested in cussing me out than describing the threat. When I finally hung up, I'd take a breath and think, I had a couple of choice words

Over time, I learned how to move around the room, doing the best I could. The hierarchy. The unspoken rules of camaraderie, when to joke, when to listen, when to speak up. How to read the room and know when silence meant exhaustion… or when it meant someone was about to break. I found ways to connect through cook-ins, potlucks, inside jokes, and desserts shared during the graveyard shift.

There's no binder big enough to walk you through every "what if" that might come through the headset. Back then, no one discussed the emotional toll. You came in, put on your headset, and got the work done. You didn't cry, at least not in public. If you had to, you ducked into the bathroom, pulled yourself together, and came back like nothing had happened. You didn't break. And you sure as hell didn't talk about the nights you couldn't sleep afterward.

When I came into the job, I carried unresolved trauma, and in some ways, it gave me an edge. I knew pain. I wasn't naïve about hurt or the darkness. I could compartmentalize. I could smile while breaking on the inside, steady my voice when everything in me wanted to scream. But what I didn't anticipate, what no one prepared me for, was the weight of absorbing other people's trauma on top of my own. Call after call. Story after story. Unacknowledged. Unprocessed. Just... absorbed.

For years, especially those first two after I was released from training, I didn't feel confident. Not. Even. Close. If I ever looked like it, I wasn't. Inside, I was constantly second-guessing myself. I didn't trust my instincts. I didn't trust my training. I didn't trust myself.

I asked for help on almost every call, not because I was lazy, but because I was terrified of missing something. Afraid of being wrong. Scared that one mistake could cost someone their life or become the call I'd replay forever. Even on the simple ones, abandoned 911s, noise complaints, fender-benders, I'd glance toward a supervisor, my voice tentative.

"Do I need to transfer this to Fire?"
"Should I keep them on the line?"
"Did I ask that right?"

The supervisors did their best. Some were patient, leaning in beside me with quiet reassurance. I can still feel the warmth of their presence at my shoulder and hear them murmur through my headset, *"Trust yourself, you've got it."* Their calm steadied me when mine faltered.

Others had less tolerance. You could hear it in the clipped tone that cut through the static when I asked for guidance one too many times. They didn't mean to be cruel; it was the nature of the job and the pressure we all lived under, but their sharpness lingered longer than they probably realized.

When I finally moved to my permanent shift, it brought a new set of relationships to navigate: supervisors, senior dispatchers, and veterans who had seen it all and wore their emotional calluses like armor. Interacting with them could be intimidating; they had the power to make your night better... or much worse.

But then there was Traci.

She carried her authority with a blend of humor and heart, her voice a mix of sass and sincerity. I can still picture her leaning back in her chair, headset crooked, one eyebrow raised as I crept toward her desk with yet another question.

"What is it now, Kris?" she'd say, half-teasing, half-amused.

She never made me feel foolish. She had a way of turning my anxiety into a teachable moment.

"What do you think you should do?" she'd ask, waiting for me to reason it out. She wanted me to trust my own judgment before I felt ready to.

Traci reminded me of a mother duck leading her wide-eyed ducklings across a freeway, calm on the surface yet fiercely protective underneath. And sometimes, that's exactly what we were: ducklings in Kevlar, waddling through chaos, trying not to get run over.

Still, my insecurities had a way of finding their way into print. Each year, my evaluation echoed what I already knew in my gut: neat lines of black ink spelling it out clearly, **Lacks confidence. Frequently asks for confirmation.**

But it wasn't performance anxiety. I wasn't afraid of coworkers listening in or of fumbling my words. It was the weight of knowing that, on the other end of that line, someone's life could hinge on whether I asked the right question or sent the right unit. If I dropped it, there was no rewind button.

Those weren't just calls. They were tests of skill, composure, and my ability to carry someone else's worst moment in my hands without letting it slip through. And I was still learning to believe I could.

I *knew* what I was doing. I'd passed the training, memorized the protocols, and mastered the systems. What I hadn't mastered was *trusting myself.* Indecision shadowed me everywhere, whispering all the ways I could get it wrong. No one needed to correct me; I was already doing that better than anyone else could.

Still, the work demanded momentum. Hang up one call, and another voice was already in my ear. Clear a high-priority event, and the next one was flashing across the screen. I learned to move fast: a steady voice and kept going, my brain staying three steps ahead. Eventually, holding it together became second nature, so natural that I almost forgot how much I'd been unraveling in the first place.

And as for closure? That part never came easy. The story didn't always end with me, yet it always stayed with me. Some nights, I'd sit at my console, eyes locked on the screen, waiting for an update that never arrived. No closure. No answers. Just the dial tone fading into the background of the room and the cold glow of the monitor daring me to be ready for the next one.

In training, they warned us: you won't always get the ending you want. They taught us how to maintain our composure, how to enter the call, and how to ask for help when needed. What they didn't teach us was how to live with the questions that never get answered.

It wasn't the screamers or the chaos that stayed with me. It was the quiet ones, the calls that went still, leaving silence in their wake. Silence that hung in the air like smoke you couldn't wave away. It was all part of the learning process in the first few years of dispatch.

If you've sat behind a 911 console, you know the bond that forms in that room. It isn't dramatic. No hero shots. No swelling music. It's quieter than that, more stubborn, a sacred silence and a glance across the room when someone's just cleared a call that took a piece out of them. A shared breath after a rough one, the unspoken agreement: we're still here.

We laughed at things that would make anyone else go pale. The guy reporting a goose attack in his front yard? Comedy gold. A coworker would slide a candy bar across the desk as if it were hazard pay for the day's worst call. "Foot Pursuit with a screamer." That's worth at least two Snickers. Coffee was lifeblood, poured and reheated until the mug itself was stained. Let the pot run dry mid-shift, and you'd swear it was an actual emergency.

Sarcasm and dark humor were our armor. Some of the funniest people I've ever known sat behind a dispatch console. That humor wasn't just entertainment; it was a matter of survival. It released the tension in the room just enough to let you breathe again, like opening a valve before the pressure built. And I mean that. We could be serious,

serious as a heart attack, when the moment called for it. But when the air got too heavy, we'd joke, just enough to keep our chests from cracking open and spilling everything we were holding inside.

Someone would hang up, mutter, "What the fuck... ugh," and the room knew exactly what that meant: whatever had just come through the headset was ridiculous, infuriating, or both. Like the night I got a 911 call about a botched drive-thru order. Halfway through my polite "Ma'am, this is not a law enforcement matter" speech, a sticky note slid across my desk: Code Red — Hold the Mayo.

We were terrible. We laughed too hard. Once it started, it snowballed. Someone would shout across the room, "Dispatch, be advised: fries are cold, send SWAT," or "Units, respond priority; they gave her Diet instead of regular." By the time the call ended, my headset cord was twisted from trying to hold back the snort-laughs.

That's how it worked. A ridiculous moment here, a sarcastic jab there, just enough absurdity to loosen the grip of the last heavy call, to shake off the weight of the hours, the politics, the people. Then the next crisis would slam into your ear. We weren't laughing at the job; we were laughing so we could keep doing it. In dispatch, that kind of humor wasn't a weakness; it was armor. The only kind that actually held.

Call taking and dispatching isn't just learning codes or keying the mic. It rewires you. One ear always tuned to urgency. One hand ready to act. Fluent in fear, fluent in steadiness. You start to hear what no one else hears. You hear the in-between.

"I'm okay," says the caller, but their breath catches, words rushing as if they're running from the truth. That's how I knew the woman with the "minor fall" was hiding in her pantry with a swollen eye and broken ribs. A pause that felt wrong came when the teenage girl said everything was fine with her "uncle" in the room, only for the line to go dead. She called back from the neighbor's yard, panting because she had gotten free, then gave her address.

Sometimes it's in the slurring, like the retired Navy vet calling, slurring his words. Not drunk, but in the middle of a stroke. Silence can scream, too. The domestic call that went quiet mid-sentence? No crash, no shout, just nothing. I sent units fast, knowing that nothing meant he'd found her.

And sometimes a whisper from a child can be louder than a siren. I still hear the little girl, maybe seven, telling me, "I can't find my mommy, and there's glass everywhere," her voice steady, leading me to the truth until we found her hiding in the bathtub with her baby.

This job? It's not just answering calls. It's translating trauma into triage. It's the art of hearing what's not said, of catching the signal in the noise, of turning raw chaos into a structured response. Over time, it became second nature, a sixth sense sharpened by years of voices, some ordinary, some unthinkable.

This call came after I had been trained in emergency medical call-taking. One afternoon, the line rang, and I answered with my usual cadence.

"911, what is the location of your emergency?"

A man's voice came back, calm and measured.

"I've cut my leg with a saw."

Straightforward. Medical. My fingers moved automatically to verify the address, confirm the callback number, and initiate the EMS call in the system. I was nearly ready to move into the standard questioning when something in his voice snagged my attention. It was subtle, a tremble buried under the calm, like a string pulled too tight.

I slowed down. "Okay... can you tell me exactly what happened?"

His answer knocked the air out of me.

"My leg's been hurting for years," he said, his tone as flat as if he were explaining the weather. "I couldn't take the pain anymore... so I used my circular saw to try to cut it off."

For a moment, my brain couldn't keep up with my ears. I stared at the screen, frozen between disbelief and the urge to double-check my hearing.

"You... you tried to cut your own leg off?"

"Yes," he repeated, and this time the weight in his voice landed like a stone. This wasn't shock talking. This wasn't confusion. He had meant to do it. He had already crossed whatever mental threshold exists between thinking the unthinkable and acting on it.

And just like that, the call shifted. What had begun as a routine medical call became something far more layered, a mental health crisis tangled up in blood, pain, and years of silent suffering. I could hear him breathing, steady but shallow. I pictured the saw still near him, the injury, the mess, and the risk that he would go further before help arrived.

It was the kind of call that made you hold your breath without realizing it, demanding you keep your voice steady while your mind raced three steps ahead. I switched tracks, shifting from injury protocol to suicide and self-harm assessment, asking questions to keep the caller talking, keep him anchored, keep him here until sirens filled the air around him instead of silence.

It's not just about training. Training gives you the framework, the script, and the boxes to check. But the real work, the work that saves lives, happens in the spaces between the questions.

It's about staying still long enough to hear the truth hiding between the lines. About catching the tiny shifts a computer can't measure: a breath that falters, a pause that stretches too long, a word that lands heavier than the rest. It's about asking one more question, even when the screen says I've done my part.

Because the difference between routine and critical can live in a single breath. A tremor. A pause.

And sometimes, the only thing standing between a life saved and a tragedy unfolding… was my voice.

Not my uniform, not a weapon, not a flashing light. Just the steadiness of my voice in someone's ear, asking the right thing at the right time, buying seconds they didn't know they had. Seconds that could mean everything.

This is one of the quiet truths about the job, the kind you only learn by living it: a call is not always what it sounds like. On the surface, it might be a burglary, a fight, a crisis unfolding in real time. But once you're inside it, peeling back the layers, you find it's something entirely different. You only start to hear that difference, to feel it, after enough hours in the chair, enough voices in your ear, enough nights when instincts are louder than the words themselves.

Like the day I picked up the line and heard a child's voice.

He wasn't more than five. Immediately, I knew this was baby talk, the kind only a parent or pediatric nurse could decipher. Luckily for me, I was fluent. I had a toddler at home and had trained my ear to every variation of "uh-oh" and "Mommy." Still, when a child calls 911, you never know whether it's an emergency or just curious little fingers pressing buttons.

I said, "Hi there, can I speak to your mommy or daddy?"

He replied, "I can't. Mommy won't wake up."

His voice cracked just enough to send a chill through me. Then he shouted, "MOMMY! Wake up! The cops want to talk to you!"

That's when I knew. This wasn't a game. If the child weren't playing, he wouldn't be yelling for her. And if she could wake up, she already would have.

"Where's your daddy?" I asked

He said, "Daddy drives a police car."

Now that got my full attention.

I flagged down my supervisor, Karla, that afternoon, and together we went to work. We didn't have a plotted address; back then, cell phones didn't ping, and this was a cell phone call. But we had tools. We ran the number through our internal database, searching for matches tied to law enforcement in the area.

Sure enough, we found one. The number belonged to one of our deputies. He had just gone on duty and hadn't been on duty long. We reached him over the radio. He confirmed it instantly: his wife had a seizure disorder.

He gave us his address. We sent an ambulance without hesitation.

He was only five years old, but that night he became a hero. His mother had taught him a simple rule: "If I don't wake up, call 911." When the moment came, he did exactly that. His voice was small, his words clumsy, but his calm was unwavering. He told me the truth, the only way he knew how.

I could have dismissed him as a child playing on the phone. I am sure many operators would have done the same thing I did. It is ingrained to listen to the subtle cues. But I listened. I leaned into his pauses, the steady innocence in his tone, the urgency tucked between words. Even at five, he had something important to say.

That's the essence of dispatch, not just hearing the words spoken but recognizing the life hidden between the lines.

It's the weight of his tiny voice in my ear.

The reminder that not all heroes wear badges.

Some wear Spider-Man pajamas and pick up the phone.

That call? That call still has a place in my heart.

I remembered being a child myself on the phone, holding my breath, trying to save my little sister and me so long ago. It was strange, guiding someone else through the fear I'd once felt so sharply.

I began to understand something no training manual, laminated ten-code chart, or neat little checklist could prepare me for: every call leaves something behind. A weight. A lesson. Sometimes, a bruise you won't even feel until much later. I was still new, still soaking up everything I could like a sponge, but I was starting to see that this job wasn't just about the calls; it was about the people you shared the room with.

# CHAPTER 4

## TRAINING WHEELS OFF

I thought I was finally finding my way behind the console, settling into the steady cadence of call-taking and discovering confidence in the chaos. It took about a year and a half, just enough time for me to think, I've got this. But dispatch has a way of sensing comfort and shaking things up.

In mid-1999, just as I began to feel settled, I decided to dive headfirst into the world of law enforcement radio dispatching. This wasn't just a step up; it was a different battlefield. Call-taking was controlled chaos, a direct lifeline between me and the caller, voice-to-voice. But radio dispatch was another animal altogether. It was a careful balancing act: juggling multiple officers, radio frequencies crackling urgently in both ears, and decoding an endless stream of signals and demands, relaying facts on a screen to the responding help, each requiring instant decisions.

Back then, training on radios was a gradual process. We began with Admin Radios, mastering the basics first, including running driver's licenses, checking tags, coordinating wreckers, and handling all administrative tasks. Even then, safety was fragile, an illusion. At any moment, if Main Radio had a high-priority incident, such as a pursuit, an armed robbery, or shots fired, the dispatcher would suddenly declare a "10-03 (Hold Traffic)," shutting down all other traffic on their channel and diverting everything to Admin Radio. In those seconds, minutes, or hours, you'd better be ready to handle a sudden influx of calls and units rushing for instructions. To a newbie, terrifying doesn't even begin to cover it.

*I remember the year I trained because, later that year, I was at Admin Radios on New Year's Eve. The circumstances were surreal, even by dispatch standards. Just a note about this evening: It was December 31, 1999, New Year's Eve, just as I was officially released from training on Admin Radios. I was nervously sitting at my console, surrounded by blinking screens, as part of the team tasked with migrating from an old, C:/-prompt-based setup to a modern Windows-based CAD system. At the very stroke of midnight, the notorious Y2K loomed overhead. Yes, you read that right: New Year's Eve and a major CAD (Computer) system change. Talk about tempting fate.*

*Around me, the dispatch floor buzzed with a mix of tension and electric anticipation. Supervisors paced anxiously. Operators traded uneasy jokes. All eyes flicked toward the clock, each passing minute feeling like an eternity. Everyone expected something, anything, to go wrong. When the clock hit 11:59 PM, the entire room seemed to hold its breath. Headsets pressed tightly against ears, eyes scanning monitors, fingers hovering over keyboards, bracing for chaos.*

*But midnight came and went quietly. Screens stayed brightly lit; radios kept humming; nothing exploded, crashed, or faltered. A collective exhale rippled through the room. For one heartbeat, relief washed over me. Then, almost immediately, the radios crackled again, snapping me back into focus. In dispatch, the silence never lasted long, especially on New Year's Eve. In dispatch, the chaos never waits long.*

Law Dispatching wasn't anything like call-taking. There was no pause, no verbal cues to prep you, no gentle ramp into crisis. It was pure, immediate, unfiltered, nonstop reaction. The stress didn't spike and fall like it did on 911 lines; it lived in your chest. I wasn't just learning incident codes or how to keep a caller calm anymore. Now I had to memorize unit numbers, tones, voices, car numbers, agency boundaries, all while staying two steps ahead of the chaos. Sarasota Police had their tempo. The County had its own. And the radios didn't wait for you to catch up. They came alive in waves, fast, relentless, unforgiving, demanding that you keep up or be swallowed whole. They could die just as quickly as they had come.

My training officers were veterans, radio gods, really. They had what we called "radio ear." It was more than hearing; it was hearing through the radio garble. They could hear exactly what the officer or deputy was saying, and to me, it sounded like an alien signal. They also knew what came next, what was coming before it was said, predicting the next move like a chess master mid-game. I was still fumbling, scribbling notes and double-checking every entry in CAD, trying to keep up with the work. The radio had a low static buzz, a kind of electric breath. And when that telltale click echoed through my headset, it meant a deputy was about to speak, and I had to be ready for anything. There were no second chances on the radio. You didn't get to say, "Wait, can you repeat that?" *You could ask them to repeat, but in training, they expected you to get it the first time,* not when someone's safety was at risk. You had to hear it the first time, understand it, acknowledge it, log it, and act on it, now. Repetition was the only way. And I trained hard, leaning into muscle memory and anticipation as my life depended on it, because someone else's actually did. There were times I couldn't breathe. Times when transmissions blurred together, traffic stops, tow requests, license checks, warrants, BOLOs, and foot pursuits. Sometimes it was quiet for hours. Other times, chaos erupted without warning.

The transition from calm to crisis never gave you a warning shot. It just hit. Then came the moments that changed everything: garbled transmissions mid-fight, a shaky voice barely spitting out a unit number, the gut-punch of knowing something was wrong and being unable to reach them. Those moments didn't just test your training; they also tested your resolve. They tested your instinct. They tested your soul. No call was routine. A welfare check could spiral into a shooting. A noise complaint could explode into a foot chase. You had to stay locked in. Eyes on the screen. Hands on the keyboard. Ready.

That kind of vigilance rewires you. The adrenaline didn't fade when I unkeyed the mic; it followed me out the door, settling into my shoulders and coiling in my gut. By the time I pulled into my driveway, my hands ached from hours of gripping the console's edge. Sleep barely took the edge off; even in the quiet of my bedroom, my mind stayed on the channel, waiting for the next voice to break through. And when I walked back in for the next shift, headset in place, it was as if I'd never left, my body already braced for the first transmission.

The training officer had my back. At least on this radio, I could jot down the requests as they came in instead of trying to hold them all in my head. At the end of each shift, we'd go over my day, what I did right, where I stumbled, and each day, the gaps got a little smaller. Slowly, I was finding my rhythm. My "radio ear" was coming into tune.

Then came the moment that felt like a turning point: after juggling multiple incidents and keeping the air clear without prompting, my training officer told me I was ready to work the Admin channel solo. What a relief.

Admin might not have been the high-adrenaline channel, but it came with its own set of challenges. Requests for tow trucks, license plate checks, warrant confirmations, and "Can you call my caller and have them step out?" were handled while logging every move, keeping the right units updated, and ensuring nothing urgent was buried under the chatter. One night, I had an officer on the line needing a rush on a warrant confirmation while two others were calling in plate numbers back-to-back, and someone else was requesting the animal control officer for a raccoon in the courthouse parking lot. It wasn't glamorous, but it was a juggling act, and for the first time, I felt like I could keep all the pins in the air without dropping one.

Even though I was on my own, I made my fair share of rookie mistakes. One time, an officer asked me to call a complainant back and have them step outside. I called, but there was no answer. Trying to sound professional, I keyed up and said, "3203, the caller advised they weren't home."

There was a pause. Then he came back with, "Dispatch, what did they say?"

That's when it hit me, I'd just reported a whole conversation with someone who didn't even pick up the phone. Mortified, I scrambled to fix it: "Correction, no answer on callback."

The main dispatcher next to me heard what I just said and started laughing. I just dropped my head, shaking it and muttering, *What the heck was that?* Another fine moment in the glamorous life of a dispatcher.

About a year later, I finally started my Main radio training.

For what felt like an eternity but was really only six relentless weeks of training, this was the big arena, the main stage. I was on the radio with deputies and officers, updating statuses, assigning calls, putting them on traffic stops, and checking their welfare, the big stuff. I was psyched… and completely terrified. This was a huge responsibility. And I was about to jump in.

The headset clamped snugly against my ears, and I sat in that chair, learning to juggle it all: dispatching deputies to emergencies and routine calls, tracking their every move, and listening for the subtle catch in a voice that meant something was wrong. One second, I was clearing a shoplifting call; the next, I was coordinating a foot pursuit, then breaking in on a car chase, or responding to a mundane parking violation. The air in my ears crackled with radio traffic, while my eyes ricocheted between CAD screens, maps, and the radio console. It was like trying to *follow six TV shows at once, each with its own plot twist.*

Over those six weeks, I rotated through multiple training officers, each with their own style, rhythm, and "right" way to do things. It was like cooking dinner with three different chefs, one after another, each insisting their method was the gold standard. I had to adapt quickly, picking up what worked and discarding what didn't, because in this seat, falling behind wasn't an option.

We ran both the police department and the sheriff's office radios, each a living, breathing network of voices that never stopped moving. Some days it felt like playing chess on two boards at once, except that every piece could move simultaneously, half of them were armed, and the stakes were life and death. My left ear would be locked on a domestic disturbance spiraling toward violence while my right tracked a routine traffic stop that suddenly went sideways. The pace was relentless at times, the margin for error thinner than a breath. One wrong word, one missed update, and the whole thing could shift against you.

Every shift, I carried the same quiet prayer: Let this be the day I get it right without being reminded, corrected, or rescued. I'd take my notes, swallow my pride, and try again. But there were nights I'd drive home with my chest tight, convinced I was destined to be the first trainee in history to wash out purely from overthinking.

When I fell behind on transmissions, the air would clog with units waiting for me to catch up, tension tightening like a noose. That's when my training officer would cut in, calm but commanding, clearing the channel and rerouting the chaos like an air traffic controller yanking a rookie's plane out of a nosedive.

They never had to be as hard on me as I was on myself. I'd lie awake, replaying every hesitation, every stumble, every "Say again?" from the field.

But progress came, painfully slow, almost invisible, like watching the minute hand on a clock. My timing sharpened. My updates flowed smoothly. My voice gained a little more authority in the chaos.

It was almost impossible to believe that just six weeks earlier I'd been a fumbling rookie, tripping over transmissions and second-guessing every keystroke. Now they were about to cut me loose on a main channel, with no safety net and no training officer shadowing my every move. It was thrilling… and terrifying in equal measure.

Complete confidence, though? That was still a distant glimmer on the horizon.

Then came the evening. Patryk looked across the console, gave a high five (figuratively, not literally), and released me from training on the Main Radios.

A little about Patryk first. He'd started a couple of months before me, back in 1998. His ID was 1479. Mine was 1489. That's how the County marked us, with numbers that would outlast our names in the system.

Patryk carried himself with quiet confidence, a steady presence, a dry Polish accent, and the kind of deadpan humor that could make you laugh mid-crisis without even realizing it. He was calm without effort, the type of person who didn't need to raise his voice to be heard.

I still remember the day he became a U.S. citizen. No big speech, no attention-seeking. Just a shy smile, his posture a little straighter, the pride understated yet unmistakable.

Patryk never wanted stripes or titles; supervision wasn't his thing. But training? That was his domain. He had a gift for seeing past someone's mistakes to the version of themselves they could become and guiding them there without ever making them feel small for not being there yet.

He'd trained me early on, back when I didn't even trust myself to type and talk at the same time. Later, when I ran the training program, he became one of my go-to field trainers, the one I could trust to take a struggling rookie and turn them into a steady operator.

He didn't chase the spotlight, but the room ran smoothly when he was in it. Patryk didn't just build dispatchers; he built people from the inside out.

That evening, Patryk released me from training in the simplest way possible. No speech. No ceremony. He just slid his chair back, gave me a quiet nod, and said, "You're good."

I knew it meant more than just passing a phase. It meant he believed I could stand on my own two feet.

I still remember my first night flying solo on Main Radio, as if it were burned into the fluorescent glow of the room. The universe, I swear, saves its best drama for after dark. Patryk stayed beside me for that first shift, not hovering, working the channel next to me, just there, his calm presence like a weighted blanket over the rising vibration of my nerves.

Our shared console pulsed with activity, a living, breathing thing made of screens, static, and the constant click of keys. I thought it would be another night of juggling calls and watching the clock. I had no idea I was about to be thrown into the deep end.

Then the first call came in: a suspicious person outside a bank. Masked. Pacing. I keyed up, my voice steady. "Any unit in the area?" because I had no units available in that area.

Nothing too alarming, at least, not yet. I told myself it was just a warm-up.

Then the second call hit.

Robbery at gunpoint.

At a local Pizzeria

Same description. Same suspect.

Suddenly, the air in the comm center shifted, like someone had cracked the seal on a storm.

"3209, 10-51 (en route)."

"3208, 10-51 (en route)."

"3210, 10-51 (en route)."

The radio lit up like fireworks, unit numbers and voices overlapping, each snapping through my headset. In the background, sirens wailed faintly, some close, some far, weaving through the static. I acknowledged each unit, stacking their calls, my fingers pounding the keyboard so fast it felt like muscle memory had finally arrived at the party.

I was still knee-deep in that one when the third call came in.

Another robbery.

At a local business

Same suspect.

This wasn't just a call anymore. It was a spree.

Then came the voice that froze the air.

"3203 to dispatch."

"Go ahead, 3203."

"I have the suspect right in front of me at the light... he's counting the money."

Time folded in on itself.

"10-03 Channel 1. All units hold traffic."

The words had barely left my mouth when the radio erupted. The chase was on. I could hear it in their voices, short, clipped, adrenaline-laced transmissions as they followed him out of our County and into the next jurisdiction. My screens lit up with unit locations, updates firing off like sparks.

Tunnel vision took over. The edges of my vision darkened, narrowing to the glow of the CAD screen and the steady thud of my heartbeat. My whole body locked into place, hands hovering over the keys, breath shallow, every nerve waiting for the next word from 3203.

"3203, in pursuit."

"Speeds forty-five... fifty... light traffic."

"Suspect eastbound approaching the Walmart University parking lot."

I could hear the tires in the background; the thrum of an engine pushed to its limit.

Then, the voice I'd been waiting for:

"Dispatch, final stop. Walmart University. I have him at gunpoint."

The air around me seemed to shrink to the width of my headset. My focus tunneled down to that one voice, that one moment. The rest of the comm center faded, with no keyboards clicking, no other calls, just me and the radio.

I didn't move. I couldn't. My fingers hovered over the keys, ready to record every word, every update. My pulse was a steady drumbeat in my ears.

And that's when I noticed it, the sweat. A slow, steady line slid between my shoulder blades, pooling at the small of my back. It wasn't just heat; it was the body's way of burning off fear without asking permission. My shirt clung to me, my jaw tight enough to ache, and still

56

I didn't let my voice waver.

Because in that moment, it wasn't about me. It was about keeping that channel clear, that officer focused, and that suspect in custody, without another voice breaking through the air.

"3203 Dispatch"

I said, "Go ahead, 3203."

"Suspect 10-15" (Suspect in Custody)

That was my baptism. My genuine welcome to Main Radio.

I thought the most challenging part was over. I hadn't yet met the silence.

# CHAPTER 5

## THE SPACE BETWEEN TRANSMISSIONS

I thought my baptism on Main Radio had been the trial by fire. I hadn't met silence yet.

Not the comfortable kind, but the kind that presses in, the space between a question and an answer, between a voice and the dead air where it should be. That's where the real fear lives.

Adrenaline? It doesn't wash off in the shower. It doesn't dissolve just because the call ends. It seeps in, staining the edges of you.

It reshapes your nervous system, training your jaw to stay tight even while you sleep. Your stomach learns to live in a constant state of tension. You're never truly "off." Just... "between."

I knew that feeling long before dispatch. The body locked and ready, the mind scanning for what might come next. It was the same tension I'd carried as a child, listening for the sounds that meant it was time to run, hide, or stay perfectly still.

The hypervigilance. After years of living with it welded to your shoulders, never setting it down, you start to forget what it feels like not to be on guard.

Little by little. Shift by shift. You give up pieces of yourself.

Whether you're dispatching over the radio or taking 911 calls, you trade those pieces away to fear, vigilance, and the unrelenting duty of being the voice when the world is falling apart.

For me, that vigilance didn't start in the comm center; it began in childhood. Long before the headset, I was already living by the rules of survival. The rules you learn when you grow up in chaos. When I had to memorize escape routes instead of bedtime stories. When I knew exactly how the air in a room changes before someone explodes, I learned to listen for danger before it had a name. To read the room before anyone spoke. To sleep lightly and wake fast.

Dispatch didn't create that in me; it just gave me a uniform and a timecard to punch.

Most people will never understand what that costs. But those of us who've lived it? We don't forget. And when it's our turn to guide the next generation, we don't just teach them the codes, signals, and CAD shortcuts. We teach them how to survive independently. How to step out of the headset at the end of the shift and come home to their own minds. How to ask for help before the job erases them, one call at a time.

Because that's the real training, and it never really ends.

Most people move through life by the rhythm of a 9-to-5 clock, a predictable, neatly divided structure of hours and tasks. But dispatchers? We live by the emergency clock. Time doesn't tick here; it pulses. It ricochets between stillness and chaos.

One moment, it's quiet. Then the bell rings, and the room erupts with urgency.

Here, time stretches, contracts, and sometimes disappears altogether. It's measured not in minutes but in moments. In heartbeats. In the breath a caller takes before answering your question. In the space between an officer calling for backup and the sound of their voice again.

Because in this world, a single second can hold a life.

And some calls distort time, seconds that unravel into eternities, where you can feel every beat of your own heart counting down.

It starts like any other radio check.

Routine. Predictable.

"Dispatch to 3210. 10-74?" Are you okay?

Radio Silence.

But that kind of silence is never empty. It's loaded. It vibrates with meaning, a low, electric buzz that pounds straight through your chest. The headset hisses, just faint enough to make me think a voice is coming, and then... nothing.

I sit up straighter. That pause? I know it. It's the one that punches fear right through your ribs.

My brain switches into triage mode without asking permission:

Did I log him at the correct location?

Who's closest to back him up?

What was he doing?

What's the vehicle description?

Did I miss something?

Then, click. His mic keys up.

Still no voice.

I don't breathe. I barely blink.

"3210, do you have traffic?"

Nothing.

A different voice breaks in, tense, clipped, too fast.

"Dispatch, what was his last location?"

"3211, he was at Tamiami and Bee Ridge," I fire back without hesitation. My fingers are already scanning CAD, flipping through unit statuses, praying for a flicker of green, anything to tell me he's still moving.

Every second is a fist around my lungs. Sweat slides down the back of my neck, sticky and cold at the same time. My stomach twists hard enough to hurt.

Is he fighting someone right now?

Is he unconscious?

Or is he just writing a damn ticket and forgot to check in?

The space between transmissions is a void, a black hole you can't escape. And the worst part? You still must sound calm, measured, and professional, as if your blood weren't boiling with dread.

Inside, though, I'm screaming:

Please say something. Just let me hear your voice.

And then, finally, and panting

He says, "3210, dispatch. 10-15." Suspect in custody.

The air rushes out of my lungs so quickly I almost feel lightheaded. I mark it in CAD, move to the next call, and my voice steadies again. But that jolt, that moment of nothing, will replay in my mind long after the shift is over.

Relief crashes through me like the first breath after surfacing from deep water. My shoulders drop. My lungs expand. The blood roaring in my ears fades back into the familiar buzz of the room. For a moment, I lean back, just a second, long enough to feel how hard I'd been holding it all in.

But the headset doesn't care. It never waits. The next call is already ringing. And I dispatch it because this is what we do. We don't get to pause. We don't get to fall apart. We keep showing up, one heartbeat at a time.

I sit up straighter, force a breath past the tightness still coiled in my chest, and reach for the next call as if it's just another thread in the tapestry of the shift. That's the job: swallow the adrenaline, steady the voice, move on.

But sometimes the residue clings. Sometimes the weight doesn't release when the call disconnects. It settles quietly in your bones, waiting for the next surge to shake it loose.

And eventually... it does.

You also have the ones sitting right beside you, your pod partners, your buddies in crime, the ones who get it. They keep you grounded and have your back. And when it's busy, when you're swamped, you hang on to each other just to survive the shift.

I'll never forget one night in the Sheriff's Office radio pod when the three of us were getting absolutely buried in traffic. Calls were stacking up, units were keying up back-to-back, and it felt like we were all sprinting just to stay a step behind. I was working the Admin Radio channel, my headset glued to my ears, trying to keep up. I can't even remember who had Main 1 (SD1), but Erik was on Main 2 (SD2).

In the middle of all that chaos, I suddenly heard a loud bang behind me. I whipped my head around to my left, and there was Erik, sprawled face down on the floor. He had passed out cold.

But there's no pause button in dispatch. SD1 couldn't stop transmitting. I couldn't stop transmitting. My radio traffic kept spilling out of my mouth while my eyes stayed locked on Erik lying on the carpet. Finally, midway through the transmission, I yelled for the supervisor.

She came over, and all I could manage was: "Umm... Erik??" She took one look and shouted across the room to the Fire Pod: "Get EMS over here ASAP. Erik's passed out!" She knelt beside him, checking for signs he was okay, while another dispatcher slid into his chair to take over his channel. The radio traffic didn't let up for a second. We were still getting hammered, with calls flying in and voices overlapping.

By the time EMS hustled upstairs, Erik was starting to come around, blinking against the light. They squeezed into our tiny pod, kneeling between chairs and consoles to assess him. The next thing we knew, they had him loaded onto a stretcher, ready to wheel him out.

And in true dispatcher fashion, Erik cracked a grin and said, "If I knew the cute paramedics were coming, I would've fainted a long time ago."

The whole room burst out laughing, the tension breaking for just a second before we went right back to the chaos on our screens. That's the strange rhythm of dispatch, one minute you're laughing at dark humor in a crowded pod, the next you're staring down the call that shakes you to your core.

Most dispatchers may relate to this moment, the one that uncovers a hairline crack in your composure, slips past your training, and stops you cold. The one scenario no academy can prepare you for, yet every single one of us remembers.

Mine came one night on the Evening Shift.

The evening shift was my favorite, from 3:00 p.m. to 11:00 p.m., when the city hummed with tension, daylight burned off into shadows, and emergencies swelled with the sunset. I loved that pulse, the steady thrum of controlled chaos. The rhythm of adrenaline is paired with precision.

But that night… something was different.

Same headset. Same CAD. Same number of officers. But the calls didn't trickle in; they crashed. One, then two, then five stacked deep. My radio lit up like a pinball machine. Units are talking over each other. Tones dropping. Calls came in faster than I could clear them.

And suddenly, I was underwater, like I was back in training, except this time there was no training officer plugged in beside me to catch me before I sank. The voices tangled in my ears, a knot I couldn't untie. My hands lagged behind my brain, a half-beat too slow. The screen blurred. My heart pounded so hard it seemed to drown out my own thoughts.

And then I froze, just for a second.

But in dispatch, a second is an eternity.

The cursor blinked at me as it knew.

The radios kept chirping, short bursts of code, clipped voices calling my name.

"Dispatch, confirm?"

"Do you have that traffic?"

"Copy, we're still holding."

Sirens coming over the radio, and I just… stopped.

My mind scrambled. What's the priority call? Who is closest? Did I miss something? But my fingers refused to move. The room spun, fast and loud, and I wasn't in it.

I forced my voice through the tightness in my throat. I asked for help, not because I'd failed, but because in that moment I knew no one survives this work alone. Not the fastest. Not the calmest. Not the strongest.

I caught my breath. Found my footing. Kept going. From the outside, it looked like nothing had happened. But inside, something had shifted.

That night didn't break me; it made me realize something. From then on, I made a promise to myself: When the chaos comes, and it always does, I will meet it not with panic but with purpose, not with fear but with focus.

People think the pressure in dispatch comes from the big calls, the bank robberies, the shootings, the ones with sirens, flashing lights, and headlines. Sure, those moments leave scars. But the real grind? It's in the quiet pressure.

It's about getting the address right the first time, every time. It's about sending the right unit when the caller's sobbing, the details are falling apart, and you're piecing the puzzle together in the dark. It's about juggling three calls, one officer screaming for backup, two 911 lines ringing, and a computer shrieking in the background. It's about knowing you cannot mess up, because if you do, someone's life could depend on it.

And here's something to think about: I didn't realize you don't get to say, "I'm tired." You don't get to say, "This is too much." You don't get to hand the headset to someone else.

You are the lifeline.

You are the calm in someone else's chaos.

And the person on the other end is trusting you with everything.

That weight? You carry it every shift. Over time, it becomes a second skin. We joke about it. We call it "part of the job." But the day you finally try to set it down, years later, you realize how heavy it was.

If I had to explain the sound of dispatch, it wouldn't be sirens or screams.

It would be the sharp, unmistakable click of a mic being keyed, the sound that means this is it.

Radios taught me more than how to push buttons and call out unit numbers. They taught me the language of survival, and it can be spoken in clicks, static, silence, and the slightest inflections most people never hear. It's the sharp, unmistakable click of a mic being keyed, the sound that means this is it.

It's the short hiss of static before a voice breaks through

"3210, I need backup now!" and feeling the air thicken, the whole room still, your heart sprinting ahead of your brain.

It's the brittle silence that follows,

"Shots fired. I have them at gunpoint."

That split second when the radio goes dead, just long enough to feel like a lifetime, and not knowing whether the next sound will be a voice… or more silence.

It's the long, hollow pause when I key up for a status check:

"3214, 10-74?" … nothing.

Again, louder this time:

"Dispatch to 3214. 10-74 check."

Still nothing. In that silence, my mind races through every worst-case scenario: Are they fighting? Are they hurt? Are they gone?

Those sounds... they live inside me.

They're not just part of the job; they become part of you. They come home with you, sure, in your thoughts, in your dreams, in the little things that suddenly feel different. The click of a seatbelt. The tone of a radio chirp. Even silence has its own presence.

And yes, over time, you change. But here's what I learned in radio training and every night since: with all that weight, all that pressure, all those invisible marks the job leaves on you, we still show up. We always show up. Because we're the ones who keep the line open, who walk people through their darkest hour, who give calm when the world is unraveling.

# CHAPTER 6

## STEADY GROUND, CRACKED EDGES

If training for call-taking and radios wasn't already pushing my emotional limits, life outside the center ensured they were tested even further. 1999 wasn't just another year; it was the year my life hit the accelerator in ways I couldn't fully see at the time.

On paper, everything was moving forward, with promotions on the horizon, new opportunities, chances to travel, and the sense that I was building something solid. But beneath that glossy surface was a constant juggling act, trying to keep every plate in the air, juggling work, home, ambition, and motherhood, praying none of them would come crashing down.

Between shifts, my girls were my center of gravity. And oh, my girls. On my days off, we escaped to the beach, far from the consoles, the tones, and the endless curve of learning that seemed to follow me everywhere. Just us, the ocean, and a quiet you can feel, the rhythmic hush of waves, the warm press of sand, and the fleeting illusion that the world could be this calm all the time.

My daughter, Kayla, with her cascade of blonde curls, was the kind of girl whose hair drew strangers to stop and admire. She'll tell you now it's a curse, but back then, people would have paid money for it.

And Linda, with her straight hair and big, curious eyes, was forever darting off as if she had urgent business somewhere. On my days off, they were my little models. I always carried my 35mm camera; this was before smartphones turned every moment into content. Back then, it was film. Intention. Clicks that counted.

We'd head to the beach, sugar-white Gulf Coast sand under our feet, the bathwater-blue ocean stretching out in front of us. I'd set up a tent near the water's edge, buckets and shovels in hand, slathering them in sunscreen thick as frosting. Kayla would dig enormous holes, beaming with pride. "Mommy, look what I made!" Linda, still in diapers, would sprint past with a shovel in one hand, a spray of sand flying from the other, as if whipping up her favorite recipe.

The ocean has a sound, a pulse, gentle and persistent. That rhythmic slosh against the shore, the chatter of seagulls overhead, carried me back to when I was their age. My mom used to take us to Lido Beach, setting us in a playpen under the whispering pines while she closed her eyes to the breeze.

One afternoon, I'd relax, sunglasses on, the warm air licking my cheeks, and I was there again, a child in the sun.

Then… SPLASH.

A bucket of salt water landed square in my lap, courtesy of Kayla. I shot up like a cat dunked in a tub, and she laughed as if it were the funniest thing in the world. I laughed too, because in that moment the memory faded and the now came rushing back. "Let's go put our feet in the water," I said. We walked to the shore and sat down, one girl on each side of me, the waves reaching for us in slow, steady breaths. It felt like the ocean was trying to wash something off me, the trauma, the tension, the stress of the headset. For a moment, I let it.

I wish we could have stayed there forever. But life doesn't freeze-frame, no matter how badly I want it to.

Dispatch had become my anchor and my battlefield.

I was still learning the unpredictable dance between call-taking and dispatching, still trying to find my rhythm on the floor, when I decided to take my girls on vacation and fly to Alaska. I told myself it was just a trip, a chance to see family, breathe different air, and show the girls something bigger than the four walls of our life in Florida. But deep down, I knew what it really was. I needed distance. I needed quiet. I needed somewhere so far away that the tones couldn't reach me.

I was struggling with the new partner in my life, with bills that never quite balanced, and with the constant worry of raising two little girls on a single income while pretending I had it all under control. Alaska became my escape hatch, my pause button in a world that never seemed to stop spinning.

That summer, we flew to Anchorage for my mom's graduation from massage therapy school. The girls were five and two, bright-eyed and endlessly curious, untouched by the weight I carried. We road-tripped north, chasing daylight that never faded. We camped under skies that refused to go dark, built fires that crackled against the chill, and stood in wildflower fields so vivid they looked like dreams you could walk through. We hiked across glaciers in shorts, our breath fogging the air that smelled of pine and freedom. Moose grazed in the distance, quiet guardians of another world.

For the first time in years, I could hear myself think. There were no sirens, no radio chatter, and no shift schedules taped to the fridge. Just my girls' laughter, the crunch of gravel under tires, and the road's rhythmic sound as it stretched endlessly ahead.

I didn't realize it at the time, but Alaska wasn't just a vacation. It was the first moment I stepped back enough to see how tightly I'd been holding everything together and how much I needed to let go.

I can still see them running through those fields, hair flying in the wind, laughter spilling into the never-ending daylight. I memorized every detail, the smell of woodsmoke in our hair, the chill of glacier air against sun-warmed skin, the flush of pink on their cheeks. That trip carved itself into my heart. For once, I felt I was doing something right.

But the quiet didn't just give me space to breathe. It gave me clarity.

Even amid all that beauty, my mind kept drifting home. The new custody agreement meant I was already missing half their lives, and being this far away only sharpened the distance.

In Alaska, I tried to picture my life without a man who would be part of my future, but no matter how far the mountains stretched or how endless the daylight felt, I couldn't erase him from it. By the time our plane touched down in Florida, the decision had settled like a stone in my chest: I'd give us a chance.

Work didn't slow down to accommodate my revelations. Every shift was a marathon, tone-outs crashing through the room, priority calls stacking up, units sliding across my mental chessboard. Somewhere in the middle of it all, I learned to wear calm like a second skin. Even if the whole floor was burning, my voice stayed steady.

But life outside the console was a storm entirely different from that. Childcare I couldn't afford. Too much income to qualify for government help, but not enough to live on. I found myself making choices I never wanted to face. On paper, they seemed logical, practical, and even responsible. But in my chest, they tore me open in ways I didn't have words for.

There's no pause button in dispatch for tears over custody agreements. The tones don't wait. The calls don't care. I answered anyway. I sent the units. I made sure everyone else got home safely. And then I'd drive to a house that greeted me with silence, a silence so sharp it echoes in my bones. I'd sit with a grief that doesn't fit into any category, a grief I can't hand off to someone else to carry. So I'd carry it alone. And I'd keep showing up, because that's all I knew how to do.

Motherhood has its own brand of grief, and this was mine: a wound that never bled but never closed. I didn't have language for it then, but I felt it everywhere, like a hollow under my ribs. After long shifts, ears still ringing with sirens and strangers' screams, I'd step into a quiet so loud it prickled my skin. No little footsteps racing toward me. No cartoons humming from the living room. Just the sound of the refrigerator and the aching knowledge that my daughters' laughter lived somewhere else.

They weren't neglected. They were loved, even spoiled, by grandparents who gave them what I couldn't at the time, slow mornings, steady routines, patience that hadn't already been spent on twelve hours of adrenaline. I had them for holidays, birthdays, and the "big" moments. But not the small ones. Not Tuesday mornings of cereal and backpacks. Not the nightly rhythm of homework, bath, and bedtime. It was those forgettable-seeming days, the ordinary ones, that left the deepest bruise when I couldn't be there.

So I carried the custody arrangement like a quiet wound. I didn't talk about it at work or with friends. I smiled when people asked about the girls and said they were doing great, while inside I counted the days I didn't have them, measuring my life in weekends and holidays, in phone calls that always ended with, "I have to go."

Over time, I learned to hold the ache without letting it spill. My paycheck barely covered rent, groceries, and gas. Childcare had always been a fantasy. Dispatch demanded everything: my focus, stamina, and voice. The calls didn't stop because I was aching. The tones didn't care that I was missing my children.

So why didn't I quit?

Because dispatch, for all its noise and demands, was the first steady ground I'd ever stood on, the rules didn't shift beneath me, and showing up meant I belonged. I told myself I was sacrificing for them, that keeping the lights on mattered more than tucking them in. Part of me believed it. The other part carried guilt like a rope that burned my hands, no matter how tightly I held it.

Instability was no stranger to me. It had been stitched into my skin since childhood, the terror of being yanked into my father's car during the kidnapping, the sound of my mother's sobs muffled by walls too thin to hide the violence, the way the air in a room could shift before danger struck, sharp and metallic, like a storm about to break. I knew what it meant to be small and powerless, to press your back against a door and pray it didn't open. Those moments etched

71

themselves deep, teaching me early that the world could tilt without warning, that safety was a fragile illusion.

So when I finally found something steady, I clung to it with both hands. My compass had been shattered so early that "right" and "wrong" blurred together. What I did know was that a steady paycheck, a job I could count on, meant something solid under my feet. Staying in dispatch wasn't just about survival; it was about proving, to myself and my daughters, that I could be dependable, that I could be the anchor I had never been given.

In some ways, I wasn't just showing up to take calls. I was showing up to prove something, to them, to the world, maybe even to myself, that I could be the kind of presence I had always needed: steady, unshakable, safe. Even if it meant my heart had to bear the cost.

But the balance was brutal. Ten or twelve hours at a stretch, a headset practically welded to my ears, my pulse syncing to every siren, every panicked voice pleading for help. The days blurred together, some pure chaos, others mind-numbingly routine. For every life-or-death moment, there were hours of thankless calls: complaints about illegal parking, neighbors arguing over trash cans, or an HOA president furious that someone's grass was half an inch too high. The extremes lived side by side, and the constant swing between them could wear you down in ways few people ever see. Then the long drive home, where the silence hit like a fist. It wasn't the soft silence of peace; it was hollow and echoing. No dishes clinking in the kitchen. No pencils scratching over math problems. No muffled giggles slipping through bedroom doors. Just me, my thoughts, and the ache of knowing those ordinary sounds were happening somewhere else without me.

I became a master of compartmentalizing. At work, I could steady my voice while a mother screamed for her child's life. But there was no manual for standing in my daughters' empty bedrooms, staring at beds made too perfectly because no one had slept in them. No training card for the way my chest caved when I opened a cupboard and found their favorite cereal still sealed, waiting for hands that weren't there.

Still, I kept showing up. To the console. To life. In the patchwork version of motherhood, I managed to balance split custody and long shifts. It wasn't the life I wanted for them, but it was the one I could hold together with the tools I had.

I told myself stability was my gift. That a roof overhead, lights that never flickered, and a fridge that stayed full mattered more than bedtime stories or whispered prayers over tangled hair. I clung to that story because the alternative, admitting they needed both and I couldn't give it, was a grief too sharp to carry. But I felt it anyway, tucked beneath my ribs like a hollow I couldn't fill.

And when that hollow grew too wide, the thoughts crept in. Did I think about suicide? Yes. Of course, I went into a dark place. There were nights I imagined driving my car into a tree, not because I wanted to die, but because I just wanted everything to stop for a minute. I was overwhelmed. Did I follow through? No. Did the cracks start to show at work? Absolutely. But I kept showing up. I was broken, yes, but I still came in, still put the headset on, still tried as hard as I could.

In dispatch, I was the calm in the storm. At home, I was just... tired. Worn thin by a life that demanded steel in one place and left me unraveling in another. I learned, maybe too late, that love isn't always measured by the moments you manage to be there. Sometimes it's measured by the moments you miss, and how deeply they stay with you.

By the end of 1999, I thought I had finally settled the questions that lingered about Jason and me. Alaska had been its own reckoning, a pause in which I'd convinced myself I understood what we were and what we weren't. When I returned, he and I slipped into something that felt like a rhythm.

Jason had transferred into Corrections, already eyeing the bigger badge and the move into law enforcement he believed would define his future. I was clawing my way up in dispatch, hungry to prove I belonged at the table, not just behind a headset. Leadership wasn't just a title I wanted; it was proof I could rise above the chaos, that I wasn't just surviving but building something.

For a while, it felt like we were aligned. Two ambitious people, side by side, walking a path that looked solid on the surface. The hours were long, the shifts unpredictable, but there was comfort in the sense that we were pushing forward together, toward careers, stability, and the kind of life I had always promised myself I would carve out of the wreckage.

When he proposed in 2000, it was in a tiny Italian restaurant, the kind where the lights glowed low, and the air smelled of garlic and warm bread. Dessert arrived, tiramisu, cocoa dust soft on top, and there, scrawled in chocolate, were the words: *Will you marry me?* My breath hitched, and tucked inside the cream was a ring, glinting under candlelight. Before I could even form the word, he was asking, and I said yes without hesitation.

For a moment, it felt as if I were stepping into the life I'd always wanted, one that looked nothing like the chaos I'd grown up in. I told myself my girls would have what I hadn't, something real, something lasting. Before Jason and I ever said our vows, reality was already pressing hard against the edges of the dream I was chasing. I told myself determination was enough, that if I loved hard enough, worked long enough, and wanted it badly enough, it would all hold together. But deep down, I knew determination couldn't stretch hours past midnight shifts. It couldn't make money multiply or repair the sharp cracks that had already begun to appear.

I hadn't faced my past, not really. I shoved it down, buried it under motherhood, work, and the desperate hope that silence meant survival. I prayed those memories would stay locked away forever, never clawing their way back to the surface. But trauma doesn't disappear just because you pretend it isn't there.

There were people in my life who didn't believe in the fairy tale I was creating with Jason. They saw what I refused to see, that old wounds don't heal on their own and that a shaky foundation will eventually collapse. But I was determined to make this work, for me, for my kids, for the story I desperately wanted to rewrite, even if it meant ignoring every whisper of doubt telling me otherwise.

We spent the next year planning the wedding, logging overtime until exhaustion became a second language. My calendar was a patchwork of shift swaps, bridal fittings, and bill reminders scribbled in the margins. Jason humored my endless bouquet ideas and fabric swatches with a patient grin, nodding along even though he couldn't tell a rose from a ranunculus. It didn't matter; he wanted me happy, and that was enough.

Life felt like it was moving forward in neat, little steps: work hard, save money, get married, and build the life we had dreamed of. Until the day the world split open.

The day before, on September 10, 2001, I was on the radio for a special detail duty as Air Force One landed in Sarasota. The atmosphere in the comm center was tense, every word intentional, every key-up part of the security chain. My voice directed units like chess moves, officers lining the motorcade route along U.S. 41 toward Longboat Key. Engines droned low, forming a well-coordinated symphony, with each patrol car in place, forming a living shield for the President's arrival.

That night, he stayed tucked away behind layers of protection. The next morning, he was scheduled to speak at Booker Middle School, where he would sit in front of our kids, read a storybook, and let cameras capture the face of a leader connecting with the next generation.

The morning started like any other, ordinary and forgettable. Until Jason burst through the door of our apartment, his face pale, his eyes wide, his breath caught in his chest.

"Turn on the TV," he said.

I did.

And in that moment, the ground shifted. The ordinary cracked wide open. The world as we knew it, the world we thought was stable, predictable, and safe enough for presidents to read storybooks in classrooms, changed forever.

From that moment forward, life blurred into a cycle of service, ambition, and survival. In November, I reactivated my Army Reserve contract, the pull of duty too strong to ignore, even as I was promoted to a dispatch supervisor. Two worlds demanded me at once, both heavy with purpose, both forged in the fire of a country that no longer felt like the same place it had been on September 10.

December brought our wedding. Not a fairy tale, not a sweeping romance, but a promise we clung to like a lifeline. We held each other with the desperation of people who believed sheer willpower could keep the darkness at bay. In that moment, it did. We built a home around cracks we pretended not to see, patching them with duty, routine, and the belief that forward motion was the same as stability.

But looking back now, I see it for what it was. What we were building wasn't forever. It was a rescue. And a rescue is never the same as love. Rescue is adrenaline. It's survival. Clinging to each other in the storm because letting go feels like drowning. And love, real love, is steadier. Something we didn't yet know how to create.

Early in our marriage, cracks began to show. We argued, not about anything major, but about minor issues that had festered in silence. When he raised his voice, I would fade away. My body stayed, but my mind drifted elsewhere, back to the place I'd gone as a kid when the shouting became too much. A place inside myself where no one could reach me. I had learned long ago that silence could be armor. It kept me safe. But it also kept me lonely.

He would yell, waiting for me to respond, but I wouldn't. I'd stare at the floor, still, quiet, unreachable. The angrier he became, the more I retreated. That only made him feel more alone, more angry, more frustrated, I think, like shouting into a void. I didn't realize it at the time, but that silence, that instinct to withdraw, was the same one that had protected me from my father, my first husband, and every fight I didn't know how to win. It was my safest place.

Six months into our marriage, I finally went to my family doctor and said, "I need help. If I don't get something, I'm going to lose my marriage." He didn't ask many questions. He just gave me a prescription to dull my emotions. I took it without hesitation. The pills didn't fix me; they just softened the edges, dulled the anxiety, and muffled the panic. They also muffled me. I thought maybe that was what being "better" was supposed to feel like: quiet, compliant, easy to love. Looking back, I can't say whether it helped or hurt. I just know I was surviving the only way I knew how, by shrinking myself enough to fit into the version of life I thought I was supposed to want.

My so-called "new life" arrived suddenly, a whirlwind of vows, titles, and transitions that felt more like juggling plates than starting fresh. A new marriage. A new last name. A new seat in the comm center. Each carried its own weight. Wearing the headset as a call taker or dispatcher was its own storm: immediate, tangible, measurable in heartbeats and radio chatter. But stepping into the supervisor's chair was different. It was a quieter battlefield, filled with invisible landmines and unspoken rules you only learn by stepping on them. The headset trained me to react. Supervision taught me to endure.

At work, I wasn't much different. I didn't start that role with a rulebook, but I did have a mentor to guide me. I stumbled often, tripped over policies, asked too many questions, and broke protocols I hadn't even known existed. I made mistakes that hurt and learned lessons the hard way. But through the fumbling, something else began to take hold, or at least I thought it did. I started building relationships, the kind that would one day support me when everything else fell apart.

Those bonds became my quiet salvation. In a world that demanded composure, they reminded me I was still human. I didn't realize it at the time, but I was laying the groundwork for something stronger than mere survival. I was building a connection. And that, more than the pills, more than the marriage, more than the title, would ultimately save me.

I threw myself into learning how to lead. I wanted to be a good leader, not just because the title demanded it, but because I had already seen the difference between those who inspired and those who crushed. I knew what it felt like to work for both.

So I studied. I bought books, stacking them on my nightstand like tools I couldn't wait to pick up. Colin Powell's *Thirteen Rules of*

*Leadership*. George Bush's autobiography. Anything that could give me a glimpse into how others had carried the weight of responsibility without losing themselves under it.

How did they make decisions when the pressure was unbearable?

How did they earn respect instead of demanding it?

How did they keep people willing to follow them into the fire, literal or otherwise?

I read with a highlighter in hand, scribbling notes in the margins and underlining lines that struck me. I carried those lessons into work the next day, putting them to the test in real time. I asked questions. I listened. I watched other supervisors closely, studying their tone, their choices, and their blind spots. Every shift became both a classroom and a proving ground.

I wasn't perfect. I stumbled plenty. But I kept coming back, hungry to improve and determined to lead in a way that lifted people rather than broke them down.

Before I could even dream of mentoring or shaping culture, I had to master the fundamentals of the job, the mechanics that no one outside the comm center even realizes exist. Not the adrenaline-soaked radio calls or the heroics people imagine, but the unglamorous, thankless tasks that made the difference between order and collapse: seating charts that determined whether a shift flowed or tripped over itself; FMLA paperwork stacked high enough to slide off the desk; payroll corrections that turned into mini-nightmares; and the eternal curse of covering sick callouts.

Minimum staffing wasn't a goal. It was a standard. Four fire dispatchers. Two PD dispatchers. Three SO dispatchers. Three to seven call takers, depending on the shift. And at least one supervisor. Each chair wasn't just a seat; it was a lifeline, a tether between chaos and help. Lose one, and the ripple was immediate: calls went unanswered, response times stretched, and officers waited for backup that might come too late.

In our world, *"we'll make do"* wasn't reassurance. It was a warning. It meant someone, somewhere, might not get help in time. And that reality sat heavily on my shoulders every time I clipped my ID badge to my shirt and stepped into the supervisor's chair.

When someone called out sick, it wasn't just a blank spot on a chart; it was a significant absence. It was my problem to solve before the whole shift unraveled. First came the call list. Days off. Early arrivals. Late stays. I'd work the phones, asking, persuading, sometimes begging. I bartered favors like currency: *"Take this one, and I'll cover you next time."*

And when the list ran dry? I had to do the thing I hated most: pull the trigger on a mandate. That meant calling someone on their only day off and dragging them back in. Or stopping someone in the parking lot, keys in hand, and telling them, *"You're not leaving yet."*

I hated the silence before the groan when they picked up the phone. I hated the way their voice flattened as soon as they realized why I was calling. We had a rotation list to keep it fair, but fairness only went so far. With fluctuating staffing, the same names kept coming up again and again. Not because I wanted them to, but because the choices were already gone.

Every mandate felt like a betrayal. Like I was asking people who were already burned out to give me just a little more of themselves, even though I knew they had nothing left to give. But the alternative, empty chairs, wasn't an option. Empty chairs meant unanswered calls. And unanswered calls meant consequences none of us could live with.

It was never personal, but I knew it felt that way. Every time I picked up the phone, I tried to soften the blow, promising a swap later, offering an *"I owe you one,"* wrapping an order in the thin paper of a favor. But the truth was, I was hijacking someone's night. Their kid's ballgame. Their dinner plans. Their glass of wine was waiting on the counter. And still, it had to be done. Because in dispatch, seconds matter, and you don't gamble with seconds.

One shift, we set a record: seven people called out sick. The flu had swept through the center like wildfire, and the few of us left were piecing together coverage with duct tape and sheer will. Every console mattered, every voice mattered.

There weren't enough people to call in; everyone was down. So we managed staffing as best we could, with supervisors doubling up, call-takers transitioning to radio, and veterans coaching rookie's mid-call. Some of us, including me, pulled sixteen-hour shifts to make it through the next four. Then, after what felt like five hours of sleep, we turned around and did it all over again.

The air was thick with cough drops, caffeine, and exhaustion. We joked darkly about Lysol being our perfume. But beneath the humor lay a quiet pride, a stubborn resilience that said, *We'll keep the line open, no matter what.*

Because that's what dispatchers do, even when the whole room feels sick, the world still calls.

Some days, it felt like my whole job was duct-taping the shift together, keeping bodies in chairs by whatever means necessary. The public never saw that part. They never knew how fragile the balance was, how much a single absence could tilt the board, or how much pressure sat on the shoulders of the person holding the seating chart.

If you trusted your people, those moments would have been survivable. Never easy, but survivable. Dispatchers notice. They notice which supervisors fight for them, who swap shifts when they can, who bend instead of breaking. And they see the ones who hide behind the title, barking mandates like orders from a throne. I made it my goal not to be one of those. I wanted to read the room. To know who was already drowning before I asked them to swim another lap. Some days, I got it right. Other days, I didn't. But I never forgot what it felt like to be on the other end of that call, hearing a supervisor's voice and knowing my night was no longer mine.

Staffing was only part of it. The other side of the job had nothing to do with seating charts or payroll. When an incident broke, the clock was merciless. You had to know *exactly* who to call and in what order: forensics, detectives, K-9, bomb squad, SWAT, hazmat. The list lived in my head like a Rolodex I could spin in seconds.

Hesitation wasn't just a mistake; it could mean the difference between solving a case and losing it.

A supervisor's ears are tuned to the whole room. You're listening to five conversations at once, none directed at you, all yours to catch. A deputy's voice goes sharp and breathless on the radio, and your hand is already reaching for the volume. A call taker stiffens, voice cracking: *"What do you mean you've been shot?"* You're plugged in before they can wave you over. Across the floor, fire tones out a second alarm, and you're already shifting channels to make sure they don't overload.

It's not X-ray vision or super strength, but it's its own kind of superpower, the ability to listen everywhere at once, filter a dozen streams of noise, and grab the thread that matters most. When you're a supervisor in dispatch, you don't just run the shift. You run the *room*. And if you're doing it right, you're not running it for yourself. You're running it for the people in it, so they can do their jobs without looking over their shoulders to see if anyone's watching them.

Getting into that rhythm took time. I studied supervisors who didn't just wear the title but embodied it. They showed up early. They were prepared. They explained their reasoning instead of hiding behind it. They set the tone, and the room followed. That kind of leadership left a lasting impression. It motivated me to rise to the challenge.

Being a supervisor meant being the go-to point for call takers, and those questions were never simple. "Hey, I've got this situation…" could mean anything. Sometimes it was a gray-area policy call, such as a suicidal subject who wasn't technically threatening anyone else but had a loaded gun within reach. Do we send SWAT? Do we send negotiators? Do we send patrol and pray? Other times, it was a procedural snag, such as when a caller refused to provide a location but insisted, "The police know where I live," or when two neighboring agencies both claimed the incident wasn't theirs to handle.

Then there were the human moments. A frazzled operator would wave me over, headset still pressed tight to her ears, whispering through clenched teeth, "Please tell me I can hang up before I lose it on this caller." Sometimes it was the chronic 911 abuser, drunk and ranting for the tenth time that week. Sometimes it was a hysterical parent screaming so loudly the call taker couldn't get a word in. In those moments, I wasn't just a supervisor; I was a mentor. I was a referee, a therapist, and a coach, all in one.

And truthfully? I didn't always have the answers. I was still learning, still climbing the mountain of responsibility while trying not to let the floor catch fire beneath me, sometimes figuratively and sometimes almost literally. More than once, I walked into my manager's office with a look that said, *'Please tell me how we handle this one.'*

Then came the briefing, an instant initiation into life as a supervisor, with no easing in and no warm-up. Every shift began with that brief performance at the front of the room. I'd come in early, gathering the night's sick callouts, patching holes in the schedule, collecting incident updates, and finishing the seating chart that determined who sat where. By 14:45, folder in hand, I'd step up with my makeshift cape and utility belt: notes, a chart, and a notepad that usually ended the night covered in frantic scribbles.

At first, the briefing felt like standing under a spotlight, with an audience silently deciding whether to applaud or boo. Dispatchers have finely tuned radar for leadership; they can sense hesitation the way a shark smells blood. Later, I learned to settle into it. I started adding a touch of humor to break the tension, a one-liner about the weather or the latest equipment glitch. Confidence eventually replaced nerves.

But sometimes it feels like you never slow down. One moment, I was in front of the room assigning consoles; the next, I was shoulder-to-shoulder on the floor, answering call-taker questions, fielding the supervisor's phone, reviewing QA critiques, untangling a payroll correction, or sliding into a console when the gaps grew too wide.

No matter how carefully I planned the day, it could be torn apart in seconds by a critical call, a foot pursuit, a brush fire doubling in size, a multi-vehicle crash with half the county rolling with lights and sirens, or worse, a chain reaction that pulled every thread at once, setting the room on fire in a way no checklist could contain.

That's what leadership in dispatch really was. Not control, but presence. Being the steady center in a room that never stopped moving.

Supervision wasn't just about knowing the job; it was about standing in the middle of a flood and learning to breathe without drowning. Information poured in from every corner: radios barking, phones ringing, voices calling across the room, and CAD updates flashing across the screen faster than my eyes could track. My job was to catch it all, sort it, prioritize it, and push it forward without missing a beat, without letting anyone else see me falter.

For a while, I thought I had found the rhythm, the balance between holding the line and holding myself together. But dispatch has a way of shifting the ground beneath you. When you think you've steadied the scales, the job tilts them again, and you're right back to scrambling, trying to keep the room from toppling with you.

# CHAPTER 7

## THE CENTER THAT NEVER SLEEPS

It's no surprise that a center never slept, not for holidays, not for storms, not for grief. We lived in the same city, and the counties we dispatched to, which meant the voices on the other end of the line were never just strangers. They were neighbors, coworkers' families, people we'd seen at the grocery store or in line at the DMV. So it wasn't abstract for us. It was real, it was human, and it landed on my nervous system differently when I recognized the streets or the voices.

While the rest of the world enjoyed family time, while children woke up on Christmas morning to see what Santa had brought, or while neighbors hunkered down through hurricanes with flashlights and candles, we were still there. People locked their doors and turned off their lights. But our room stayed lit, a constant cadence of voices, radios, and tones that never paused.

The world outside could flood, burn, or fall apart, but inside we stayed steady, headset to headset, carrying other people's worst days. The room itself became timeless: no windows, no seasons, just the eternal glow of monitors and the rhythm of incoming calls. Some nights, the weight of it nearly broke us, pressing down until even laughter felt impossible. Other nights, laughter was the only thing that saved us, the thin thread keeping us human when the calls stripped everything else away.

But always, we kept going. Because the center never slept. And neither did we.

Holidays in dispatch were a strange contradiction. On the walls, someone always taped up paper turkeys or dollar-store garlands, desperate to inject festivity into a place that ran on fluorescent lights and caffeine. Potluck dishes filled the breakroom, with crockpots of chili, trays of cookies, and sometimes a lopsided cake with "Merry Christmas Day Shift" scrawled in frosting. We'd exchange paper plates and plastic forks as if it were a family dinner. We were a family, in our own sort of way.

Thanksgiving told the story best. While most families clinked glasses and passed plates, our phones lit up with a different kind of feast. Uncle Bob drank too much and swung at his brother-in-law. Aunt so-and-so ate until she swore indigestion was a heart attack. Dad took out the trash and wound up in the ER with a broken foot. Meanwhile, I was dispatching paramedics with one hand and trying not to spill cranberry sauce on the CAD keyboard with the other.

Mornings were eerily quiet. The turkey was still in the oven, the roads were nearly empty, and everyone behaved, at least until the wine kicked in. We sat at our consoles in the hush, daring not to speak the cursed words. *"It's quiet."* That was the fastest way to summon disaster. Our plates of turkey and mashed potatoes sat beside the monitor, cooling too fast. By the time we got a forkful, it was lukewarm at best: Thanksgiving à la dispatch.

Afternoons brought the warm-up acts, runaway cousins, teenagers puking from sneaked shots, and parents panicking over "alcohol poisoning." By nightfall, the real "holiday spirit" arrived. Old grudges boiled over with the pumpkin pie. A wife whispered from a locked bathroom as her husband's rage exploded after the third round of whiskey. Brothers settled scores in the driveway while their children watched from the porch. And the bars? Nobody was singing carols as we dispatched units to break up brawls in the parking lot.

Then came Black Friday. If the stores were open, the calls came in faster than the sales. People fought over parking spaces as if they were Super Bowl tickets. A shopper cut in line, and suddenly aisle nine turned into WrestleMania. Someone "accidentally" grabbed two flat screens, and security called us because the crowd was ready to riot. Chaos wrapped in fluorescent lighting, the unofficial sequel to Thanksgiving dinner.

**Oh, Christmas Tree,** Florida Decembers never felt like a "White Christmas." Palm trees wrapped in twinkling lights, eighty-degree afternoons, and humidity didn't exactly set the mood. So inside, we made our own magic.

The Sheriff's Office hosted a decorating contest every year, and our comm center went all out. One year, our theme was "Santa Got Run over by a Reindeer." With a lot of help, we transformed the massive, carpeted walls into a high-speed chase scene, complete with aluminum foil stop sticks and black skid marks. Every radio pod had its own paper cruiser, marked PD, SO, or Fire Truck. Caution tape wrapped around consoles, turning them into crime scenes.

The masterpiece was our spoof newscast, "*COPS: Christmas Edition.*" Christine and I played reporters 'Annie and Ally" (an inside ANI/ALI joke), reporting live as deputies tackled a runaway Santa, tased him (sound effects included), and stuffed him into the back of a patrol car. It was ridiculous, hysterical, and exactly the kind of laughter we needed. Needless to say, we won that year.

But the phones didn't care whether there was tinsel on the walls. They didn't care whether our COPS skit had us doubled over in laughter. They kept coming in: stolen-Christmas-light reports, mistletoe fistfights, and once, a man who swore his neighbor's inflatable reindeer was "looking at him funny." Festive, in its own special way.

We ate our baked ham lukewarm, laughed until our ribs ached, and carried calls that broke our hearts, sometimes all in the same hour. That was holiday dispatch: not the life we wanted, not the home we missed, but the only way we knew to keep showing up as the world outside fell apart.

Hurricanes didn't just show up one year; they lined up, as if waiting their turn, each with its own personality and its own mess to make. Ivan, Charley, Frances, Jeanne… four names burned into our memories. By the time the third one spun toward us, we moved through the drill on autopilot.

Packing for a hurricane shift felt like a twisted version of summer camp. You threw together a "go bag" of uniforms, toiletries, and enough food to last twelve hours on, twelve hours off. Except camp meant sleeping under a desk, brushing your teeth at a bathroom sink while the building rattled, and eating protein bars that tasted like drywall. Coffee was powdered, bitter, and strong enough to strip paint, the only fuel keeping us upright. The air in the comm center thickened with a scent that never left: wet ponchos drying in the hallway, stale coffee, and the tang of pure, uncut stress.

At home, you boarded up your windows and doors, tucking your house in for a fight you couldn't stick around to see. Then you hauled your bag back to work, carved out a corner of the pod for your pillow, and stashed your snacks in the bottom drawer. The center became its own storm shelter, filled with employees, voices, anticipation, and static. Elbow-to-elbow, we watched weather models, side-eyed the radar, and prayed Jim Cantore wouldn't land on our beach, the meteorological version of the grim reaper.

The phones never stopped.
"Where can I get sandbags?"
"Will they force us off Siesta Key?"
"What happens if I stay?"

Then came the line we all dreaded delivering, the one that broke hearts on both ends of the call: *"Due to weather conditions, all first responders have been pulled from the roads. We cannot send anyone until it is safe to do so."* You learned to say it flat and steady, even when the caller was begging.

Not every call was a tragedy, though. Hurricanes brought their own brand of strange. Deputies were sent to break up hurricane parties, where half the guests were drunk, dancing in the driveway, and the other half were already fighting. There were impromptu tornado touchdowns, trees ripped out like weeds, and roofs peeled back like sardine lids. And then, because the storm wasn't enough, came the rooster.

A deputy once radioed in, requesting "animal control." A rogue rooster was terrorizing a parking lot, running circles around traffic as if it owned the place. Karla, deadpan on the radio, started *clucking*. The room erupted. We nearly fell out of our chairs, half from exhaustion, half from disbelief.

Another caller asked where he could find a snow shovel in Sarasota in August. We laughed until our sides hurt. Before I could even form a response, a sticky note slid across my console: *"Code White — Shovel Recovery in Progress."*

Moments like that, absurd and ridiculous yet perfectly timed, reminded me why I stayed. The laughter didn't erase the heaviness, but it carved a small window through it, just enough to let us breathe again before the next call dropped.

After Hurricane Charley ripped through a year earlier, Kim and I drove to Charlotte County and walked into their storm-battered center, which looked like a war zone. The conference room ceiling had collapsed, the air reeked of wet insulation, and cables dangled like jungle vines. Yet on a whiteboard in the corner, someone had scrawled a shift schedule in marker. People showed up. Headsets went on. Calls got answered. I slid into a chair, put the headset over my ears, and took calls so others could go home and face whatever pieces of their lives the storm had left.

Two decades later, I'd spoken with directors in Louisiana, and they'd tell me, through tears, how, during Katrina, they loaded their people into military trucks, leaving dispatch and the 911 phones still ringing because staying would have killed them all. "But what about the calls?" one said to me, eyes glassy.

That's the thing, no matter how bad it gets, we think about *them*. The public. Our duty to serve. And we care about each other.

And sometimes... we even laughed.

One night, a storm veered at the last minute, sparing us a direct hit, though the winds outside still had teeth. During a rare lull, my Ops Supervisor, Carol, and I stepped outside to gulp some "fresh" hurricane air. As soon as the door opened, gusts slapped us, as if Mother Nature herself were shoving us back inside.

That's when I spotted it, a bright yellow poncho, the cheap kind that clings like static and makes you look like a walking banana peel. Naturally, I put it on. Hairbrush in hand, I struck my best Jim Cantore impression.

"Reporting live from the heart of the hurricane!" I yelled into my fake mic, leaning into the wind as my poncho whipped over my head, like the storm was trying to pants me on live TV. Carol doubled over laughing, phone out, filming my ridiculous one-woman weather segment.

I staggered across the parking lot, yelling, "We're losing control out here, Carol! Tell my family I love them!" before pretending to be knocked into a bush. The video, our "Weather Report," likely still exists on an old phone somewhere. God help me if it ever resurfaces.

Amid the stress, the danger, and the calls that left knots in your gut, those ridiculous moments kept us breathing. We rode out every storm the same way we rode out the shifts: together, braced against the wind, finding just enough humor to keep from breaking.

That moment, ridiculous, silly, and soaked with hurricane air, broke the heaviness. Because sometimes, when the world is falling apart outside, and you're one 911 call away from heartbreak, the only thing that saves you is letting yourself act like a total goofball for five minutes. And I loved that version of myself, the one who could be a supervisor by day and a storm-chasing clown by night. Because sometimes laughter was the only thing louder than the pressure we carried.

# CHAPTER 8

## RELATIONSHIPS

This brings me to relationships. Relationships are integral to a dispatch center, not just helpful but essential. As I grew into my role as a supervisor, I leaned into mentorship. I welcomed recruits, encouraged new hires, and made a point of building trust across shifts. Along the way, I also learned something else: laughter matters. It's a survival tool. A pressure valve. A bridge between calls that could shatter a person if they didn't have somewhere to land.

One night stands out. It was a full moon, and anyone who's worked in public safety knows what that means. The shift hadn't even hit its peak yet, and the call log already looked like something out of a sci-fi thriller. We'd taken a report from a woman convinced "little green men" were dancing on her outdoor AC unit. It was only 8 p.m., and we were already in the deep end. I broke the tension the only way I knew how: with a bit of ridiculousness. I grabbed some aluminum foil from the breakroom cabinet and went to work. In five minutes, flat, I'd constructed an elaborate, pointy-topped tinfoil hat, a real beauty. I perched it squarely on my head and strutted back into the room as if it were part of the uniform. "This," I declared, gesturing to the shiny masterpiece, "is to ward off the moon madness and the intergalactic trespassers. You're welcome." Laughter erupted across the floor. Even the most stoic faces cracked smiles. For a moment, the tension lifted, and we all breathed easier. Eventually, I slipped back into supervisor mode, working through paperwork, answering questions, and coordinating resources as needed. I'd forgotten I was still wearing the hat.

Until I heard a throat clear behind me. "Ahem… excuse me." I turned, still mid-keystroke, and there he was, the Emergency Manager. In a pressed shirt, holding a clipboard, and wearing the world's biggest grin. "Well," he said, eyes twinkling, "looks like you're having an interesting night." I yanked the foil hat off my head as if it were on fire. "Oh, Lord…" I muttered, adjusting my posture, trying to pretend I hadn't just been conducting interstellar defense operations under fluorescent lighting. He laughed. I laughed. And honestly, the entire room did, too. A little embarrassment was a small price to pay for the morale boost it gave us all that night. Because in a room where heartbreak, chaos, and adrenaline are constant companions, sometimes it's the laughter that keeps you sane.

A day in dispatch was always easier when you had a work husband or a work wife. Someone who was part comic relief, part therapist, part heavy lifter, the one who made the impossible shifts survivable. These weren't romantic relationships. They were built on loyalty, humor, and the kind of trust that only comes from sitting side by side for thousands of calls and thousands of hours.

I had two of them, at different points in my career: Bill and Dan.

Bill was everyone's go-to work partner. Whenever someone needed support, Bill was there. His infectious laugh could break even the most awkward quiet moments. Friendly and thoughtful, Bill seemed to always sense when you might need help. He'd pick up your coffee during his break or slip a Snickers onto your desk when you were having a tough night. Bill stood up for those who were new or struggling and would quietly cover your radio so you could step away after a difficult call. He made sure people felt valued. In an environment where "thank you" is rarely heard, that kindness truly mattered.

Dan arrived on the scene a bit later, but we found our own ways to connect. When I was freshly divorced, he came with his truck to help move my washer, dryer, and boxes into my new apartment, keeping things light with jokes so I wouldn't break down in front of him. At work, if things got hectic, he'd quietly lean over during a tense call and say, "You've got this," grounding me more than he probably knew. Dan always stayed out of the center's drama, gossip, rumors, and office politics. He had a reliable calmness, as if no matter how tough things got, he wouldn't let you sink. Because he was tall, we relied on him for anything out of reach, hanging Christmas decorations or grabbing items from high shelves. He even volunteered to wear the Red-E-Fox costume at public events. Whatever needed doing, Dan was always ready.

With both Bill and Dan, it was give-and-take. They weren't just rescuers; they let me be that person for them, too. We celebrated each other's wins, from passing certifications to small life victories like babies or grandbabies, and from sons winning football games to their shared kinship with a sports team. We were there for the downs, whether it was a messy breakup, family problems, or just a bad run of shifts. Sometimes that meant talking it out over late-night food in the fire pod. Other times, it was a simple nod across the room that said, *I see you. I've got your back.*

Having a work husband didn't erase the weight of the job, but it made it lighter. They were reminders that you didn't have to carry it all alone, that even behind the headset, where the world expects you to be endlessly strong, it was okay to lean on someone else.

Maybe that's why those bonds stick with you long after the job ends. They weren't just work husbands. They were proof that even in a room filled with chaos, you could still find family.

The thing about laughter is that it never lasts long in dispatch. The tones always cut it short, and sooner or later, the darkness comes back around.

Building relationships with the other supervisors at the center came naturally. We worked side by side every day, running the shift together. We bounced ideas off each other, covered shifts when someone needed a break, and traded stories about our lives outside the headset. We talked about kids, weekend plans, and the little dramas that unfolded between calls. And when health problems started creeping in for one of us, we noticed. We asked. We worried.

Not every memory from those years is light. One of our evening shift supervisors' deaths stands out to me. One minute, he was leaning over my console, laughing about shift drama and teasing someone about bringing in better snacks. The next, he was gone, with complications after surgery. His wife called 911. *Our* 911. Cardiac arrest. Not breathing. No pulse.

It was the kind of call we handled every day, the kind where muscle memory and protocol take over before the truth can sink in. But this time, the name on the screen was one of ours. Jenni, one of his best friends, was in the fire dispatch seat when it came through. After she dispatched the call, she froze, her voice breaking as she said to me, "I can't do this." Her eyes were wide, already filling with tears, and her whole body was trembling.

"Go," I told her.

She slipped off her headset and walked away, and I stayed. I watched his last moments unfold on the very screens we'd shared for years. The same system that had been our home became the place where I watched him leave it. That night, the glow from the monitors felt colder, the air heavier, as if the room itself understood what we had lost.

Holly O. wasn't just another supervisor; she was one of those rare souls whose presence could steady an entire room. We worked side by side for years, sharing shifts, stories, and those quiet in-between moments that made the chaos bearable.

When I learned she had cancer, it hit hard. It didn't seem fair, someone so full of light, compassion, and quiet strength being forced to fight that kind of battle. Watching her go through it was difficult, but even then, she carried herself with grace, humor, and warmth that never faded.

I still remember the countless hours we spent in the supervisor's position, talking about work, our families, and life beyond the center. Holly had a way of making even the longest nights feel a little lighter, reminding everyone around her that kindness still had a place in the world. I miss her.

Grief has a way of stacking itself quietly, one loss on top of another, each one leaving its own mark. Just as we were learning to find our footing again after losing Trip and then Holly, another unexpected call came through, this time from my own family. It wasn't tragic, just one of those moments that stops you for a second, reminding you that life outside the center doesn't pause for us either.

When you live and work in the same place, the lines between your job and your family blur in ways you can't prepare for. I was on an overflow 911 call, handling calls from an earlier afternoon accident, when another crash came in. In the background, I could hear a woman crying. The witness on the line was breathless, describing the scene: one vehicle overturned, the driver trapped, and looking hurt. The other driver had stumbled out of her car; the witness thought maybe she'd been drinking.

I sent Fire and EMS to the scene and hung up. Almost immediately, my cell phone rang. The screen lit up: *Mom.* I usually didn't answer on shift, but something in me said to pick up.

The second I did, my stomach dropped; it was the same crying I'd just heard in the background of that 911 call. My whole body went cold, adrenaline flooding every nerve.

"Mom? What happened?" I asked, already knowing.

Her voice was shaky, ragged. "Someone hit me... my car overturned... Krissy, I'm hurt." She is the only one in the world who has ever called me "Krissy".

I swallowed hard, keeping my voice steady. "Mom, we've got people on the way. Don't worry mom, we'll take care of you. Help is coming."

She was crying, sobbing so hard it broke something in me. Despite having all the tools and protocols at my disposal, I felt helpless in that moment.

I walked over to the fire dispatcher, the one working the very accident I knew she was in, and said quietly, "That's my mom. She's injured. Give me an update as soon as they're on scene."

Then I sat there, headset on, pretending to breathe normally, waiting for someone else to come to my *mom's aid*.

In dispatch, our lives tangle together in ways most people will never understand. We don't just work side by side; we live side by side. We throw baby showers in the break room, where we string streamers between consoles. We pass around slices of cake for bridal showers, even for the guys. We celebrate weddings, adoptions, and new homes. We've been there for each other's milestones, standing in line at the hospital nursery window, crowding into a living room for a housewarming, clinking plastic cups of punch over someone's engagement. We get close. We have to. This job welds you together.

But then… the suicides. They cut through everything. Sometimes it was an officer. I remember having to call the Chief of police to let him know one of his own had taken his own life, and he needed to respond out. Sometimes a friend or family member, sometimes another dispatcher, perhaps not in our center but still one of us. The calls were different when it was one of our own. This job is so hard, and sometimes we feel unseen. I couldn't imagine why some didn't think they could turn to one of us.

Loss didn't always come from death. Sometimes it was the kind you can't put in a report.

I've watched people walk out of this job because the silence after the calls was heavier than the calls themselves. It wasn't just the calls, it was the long days, the mandatory overtime, the holidays, and weekends spent under fluorescent lights instead of with family. The stress that grinds on you until it feels like part of your DNA. For some, it's relentless in a way they couldn't handle..

Some of the people leaving came suddenly, others quietly. Sometimes people leave not with sirens and headlines, but in silence, disappearing mid-shift, never coming back.

Some left in the middle of a shift, like the recruit who went to lunch one afternoon and never came back, their console still lit, the last call frozen on the screen. Others just... faded. One day, their headset was there, the next it wasn't. No party. No goodbye. Just an empty chair and a name nobody wanted to say out loud.

And then there were moments that hit you hard, like the day we found an operator slumped against the bathroom wall, eyes glassy and barely aware. She hadn't returned from break, so we stepped outside the center to look for her and found her on the tile floor, disconnected from herself in a way that made the whole room go still. The job had been wearing on her for months, but none of us realized how deep the cracks went until that moment. Whatever she was using to cope had shifted from "getting through the shift" to something far more dangerous. And it had clearly been building longer than anyone wanted to admit. I remember the heavy, sinking feeling that this place could break people quietly, completely, if they didn't have somewhere to put what they carried.

Some coworkers blew off steam with humor, others with a drink after shift, and everyone had their own coping mechanism.. And some... just didn't come back from it.

Because this job isn't just about the calls. It's about who you share them with, the people who can tell by the set of your shoulders that you're barely holding it together and sit with you in that silence anyway. The glances across the room that say *I've got you.* The dark jokes that pull you back from the edge. The quiet "You good?" when they already know the answer.

That's what kept me coming back. Not the headset. Not the procedures. Not even the purpose.

The people.

Always, always... the people.

# CHAPTER 9

## LEARNING THE OTHER LANGUAGE

So I was eager to stretch my horizons, started training in EMD (Emergency Medical Dispatch) and Fire Dispatching, and was determined to master every branch of the emergency response tree.

Now it was time to start learning EMD, spending four solid weeks sitting with a training officer, headset on, and learning the protocols step by step. Cardiac arrest. Severe bleeding. Long fall versus short fall. I'd sit there taking call after call, the training officer plugged in beside me, listening to every word, and, like always, I'd look for that little nod or "good job" to know I was getting it right.

The training officer sat beside me, silent but always there, listening to every word I said. Sometimes I could feel their gaze more than I heard their voice. When the call ended, I'd wait for that slight, quiet nod, that unspoken approval that meant *I got it right.* It's funny how even after years in the chair, that need for validation never really fades.

Being a supervisor didn't earn me a shortcut. Behind that headset, rank meant nothing. I was just another trainee, taking directions, absorbing critiques, and reminding myself to stay teachable. Respecting the process wasn't just about professionalism; it was about humility. Because in this line of work, every new skill could be the difference between life and death.

One of my trainers was Kelvin. He'd been doing fire dispatch since I was in diapers. The man was a legend, the kind of person who could run a fire channel in his sleep, who had the respect of everyone from rookies to the fire chief. He was humble, steady, unshakable. And I got to learn under him. I knew I was in good hands.

**Short Note about Kelvin:** *Shortly after he retired, I believe after COVID, I learned that he had passed away, and my heart broke. Thirty years in this profession is an incredible achievement for anyone, but especially for someone from his era. He witnessed more change in this field than most of us could ever imagine. Kelvin wasn't just a dispatcher; he was a legend. His calm, his humor, his steady hand set the standard for so many of us who followed. May he rest in peace. His legacy lives on in every one of us he trained, guided, and believed in.*

I had been taking calls for a bit, and then it happened, my first Cardiac Arrest call. The caller's voice trembled as she answered my first question.

"Is he awake?"

"No."

I jumped into protocol, heart pounding but voice steady.

I continued with asking questions, "I want you to listen to me carefully. Lay him flat on the ground. Put one hand on his breastbone, the other hand on top, and push down hard and fast. I'm going to count with you."

And we went, one, two, three… steady compressions, her breath quickening, my voice pushing her forward. I kept encouraging her. "You're doing great. Keep going." Four minutes later, paramedics were on scene.

I hung up, looked at Kelvin, and out of nowhere, my eyes filled with tears. I set my headset down and walked out of the room before I lost it completely. I didn't even know what hit me at first: the finality of life, the rawness of hearing the panic in her voice, the weight of knowing I had been her lifeline in those minutes before help arrived.

I came back after composing myself. Walking someone through how to save a life hits different the first time you do it. It's a kind of intensity that gets under your skin and stays there.

By the time I started (EMD) medical call-taking, I'd already been a call taker for ten years. I knew my way around law enforcement and fire calls, but medical was a whole new language. Protocols. Scripts. Step-by-step instructions where every second mattered.

After processing call after call during training, I finally started to find my rhythm. Each one felt like a new test of nerves, *control bleeding*, *seizure protocol*, an *ill person*, and *difficulty breathing*. The scenarios ran together in a blur of adrenaline and repetition, but each voice on the other end was different. Each one mattered.

The only way to get used to it was through hands-on experience; no simulation or script could teach you how to steady your breathing while someone else was losing theirs. Under Kelvin's guidance, I learned the rhythm of the call, the tone of calm, the pacing, and the confidence that made strangers trust me. He'd hover just behind me, silent but present, ready to step in if I froze. He never did it for me, though. He wanted me to feel the weight of it, the responsibility, and to find my footing in it.

The first time I guided someone through controlling bleeding, my hands shook so badly I could barely flip the card. The caller's voice was trembling too; her husband had cut his arm on broken glass. Blood was everywhere. She was panicking, saying she couldn't look. I remember hearing Kelvin's voice behind me, calm and steady: 'You've got this, Kris. Just slow it down."

And so I did. I guided her through it, applying direct pressure with a clean, dry cloth and keeping him still. The tone in her voice shifted from panic to focus, as if she borrowed my calm for a moment. That's when it clicked, just how powerful tone alone could be.

Then there was the seizure call. The mother's voice was sharp and frantic, cutting straight through your chest. "He's shaking! Oh my God, he's not breathing right!" I flipped the card, *Seizure.* I could hear the child in the background, the thud against the floor. "Okay, ma'am, don't hold him down. Move everything away from him that he could hit. Stay on the line with me." The words came automatically, but my heart was pounding. I listened for that first deep gasp, the sign the seizure had broken. When I heard it, I almost cried with relief.

And then came the *ill person* calls, the quiet ones that sounded routine but never felt that way. An elderly man alone, dizzy and sweating, insisting he didn't want to "bother anyone." The woman who said she "just didn't feel right," and something in her tone made me keep her talking until EMS arrived, she was having a heart attack.

Each call was its own world, a crash course in empathy, chaos management, and grace under fire. Some days, I'd handle a dozen calls and barely breathe between them. The rhythm was relentless: answer, assess, document, and yet somewhere in that repetition, I started to feel steady.

I wasn't an expert by any means, but I could hold my own. I could guide someone through control bleeding, tell a mother how to handle her child's seizure, or keep a lonely voice company until the ambulance arrived outside. I learned to trust the process and trust myself.

When Kelvin finally said, "You're ready," it hit me harder than I expected. Because I was. Nervous, yes. But ready.

That first medical emergency call I handled alone, the one where no one was watching over my shoulder, I still carry it with me. No amount of training truly prepares you for the moment when that headset feels heavier than usual, when you realize *you* are the calm now. And once you find that stillness amid chaos, there's no unlearning it. That's the moment you stop being a trainee and start being the voice that holds someone's world together.

That was the moment it became real.

After completing medical call taker training, I was ready to dive straight into fire dispatch. As a shift supervisor, I wanted to ensure every box was checked. If I were going to evaluate my squad fairly, I needed to understand every seat they sat in, not just from the outside, but from inside the pod with the headset on.

Between finishing the EMD training and getting my schedule to train Fire Dispatching, I would sit in Fire Dispatch taking medical calls to refine my skills. Kelvin and I would meet again, sitting side by side in the fire pod, waiting for the next call to come in. Between him dispatching and me taking calls, we filled the silence with small talk, the weather, weekend plans, and, inevitably, food. Somehow, the conversation always came back to Columbia Restaurant. "Oh my gosh," I'd say, "the 1905 Salad, the Cuban sandwiches, that sangria..." and Kelvin would roll his eyes and laugh because I'd wax poetic like we were about to detour to Lido Beach to eat. If you've ever been near Tampa or Lido and haven't been to Columbia, don't think of it as a suggestion; it's a requirement.

Fire dispatching, though, was a whole different beast from law enforcement. Firefighters weren't prowling the streets like deputies, stumbling across chaos on their own. They were in their stations, drinking coffee, polishing trucks, doing drills, playing cards, waiting for *us* to drop the tones. Structure fires, brush fires, medical calls, the occasional lift assist, and even the infamous stubbed toe. We laughed about how law enforcement had trouble *finding them*, while in the fire, the problem didn't start until *we* lit up the channel.

"Law guys are magnets," Kelvin would joke. "If nothing's happening, give it five minutes, they'll stir it up behind a Target or a Circle K." And he wasn't wrong. Deputies seemed to sniff out fights in parking lots the way sharks sniffed out their next meal.

In fire, the rhythm was different. The quiet could stretch long, filled with chatter and the low hum of the room, until, *BEEP BEEP BEEP BEEP*, the tones shattered the calm, and suddenly it was game on. I was still only trained for medical calls at that point. I could take the calls, work through the script, and give CPR instructions, but I couldn't dispatch units yet. That would come soon. And when it did, I knew I'd be the only supervisor in the room fully cross-trained in law enforcement, fire, and medical, the trifecta. Ambitious? Absolutely. But for me, this wasn't about chasing a headset and a title. I wanted mastery.

When the schedule for my **official** fire dispatch training was finally released, I was buzzing. This was it. I already knew how to run a law radio, but fire? Fire was its own language. Everything was backwards. In law enforcement dispatch, you'd say: *"Dispatch to 3203."* In fire, it was flipped: *"R23 from Dispatch."* It took conscious effort to keep my tongue from twisting the two together.

And timing? Timing was everything. Miss the rhythm by half a beat, and you could confuse a roomful of firefighters, or worse, delay a response when every second mattered.

The tones would drop, sharp, urgent, impossible to ignore, and you had seconds to get it right.

**BEEP. BEEP.**

"Engine 1, Rescue 1, respond. Chest pains. A house on Bougainvillea Street."

No wasted words. No dead air. Rule number one: the call can't hang in silence.

In under three minutes, the chain had to fire off like clockwork:

The call taker answers, enters the details, and shoots it to dispatch.

The dispatcher tones the correct station, rigs acknowledge, and wheels hit the pavement.

"Engine 1, Rescue 1, acknowledge."

"Engine 1, Rescue 1 en route."

"Copy, Engine 1, Rescue 1 en route."

While they're on the road, the updates keep coming: *30YOF C/O CP* — thirty-year-old female, complaining of chest pain. Four minutes later:

"Engine 1, Rescue 1 to Dispatch, on scene."

"Copy, on scene."

Then, "At patient."

"Copy, at patient."

Every word mattered. Every handoff had to be clean. It was like conducting an orchestra where missing a beat didn't mean a sour note; it meant seconds lost, and seconds could cost a life.

Some calls were straightforward: flu symptoms, lift assists, and transport to the hospital. But then came the monsters: two-alarm structure fires, where tones dropped like hammer blows. Suddenly, you were paging three or four stations at once, moving crews to TAC or Command channels, calling in mutual aid, and juggling coverage for the rest of the county so no one was left without backup.

I'll never forget one of my first structure fires. The CAD filled with flashing red boxes; alarms stacked so fast my screen looked like it was short-circuiting. "Engine 3, Engine 5, Ladder 2,..... etc. respond." My voice stayed steady, at least I think it did, while my heart tried to pound through my ribs. My trainer sat beside me, nodding silently, letting me sweat it out. The firefighters on the other end? Calm as saints. "Copy, en route." "Dispatch, we'll take command." Their calm anchored my panic, even as my fingers flew.

We dispatched five different fire agencies back then, each with its own thick binder of policies. Some of the rules lined up; others contradicted each other completely. The seasoned dispatchers could rattle them off without breaking a sweat. Me? I was still fumbling, flipping tabs, whispering to myself, *Please don't screw this up.*

For the next nine weeks, I rotated between the four fire dispatch positions, living and breathing fire calls. No two days were alike. The day shift had its rhythm, medicals, lift assists, and the occasional kitchen fire. Evening shift was a different animal: more crashes, more alcohol, more chaos. Each time I dropped the tone, it got a little easier, my voice steadier, my timing sharper.

When the phones were quiet, my training officer would quiz me relentlessly. Policies. Procedures. Which unit covers which area? Which agencies wanted to be paged first? I had to rattle it off from memory, like multiplication tables, without notes or hesitation.

The tones themselves were a world unto themselves. On the radio panel, the buttons were lined up by district: North, Central, South, North Port, and Englewood. At the very top sat the big one, the All-Station Tone. That button was sacred. You used it only for countywide announcements or truly massive incidents where every station needed to be listening.

Well… one day, in all my rookie glory, I aimed for Station 23 and fat-fingered the All-Station button instead.

The tones dropped across *every* station in the county. Dozens of speakers came alive at once, and there I was, loud and clear, announcing a single call meant for one *tiny* station.

Confusion rippled instantly across the radio. "Dispatch, did you mean to tone us out?" another station asked, their voices more than a little amused. Others chimed in too, some chuckling, some grumbling. A few treated it like I'd just sent the whole county into DEFCON 1.

I wanted to crawl under the console. Admitting my mistake over the radio was mortifying, the kind of rookie slip that sticks to you like a bad nickname. For a while, some crews teased me about it every chance they got: *"Careful, don't let her near the All-Station button!"* Others acted like I'd unleashed the apocalypse. Either way, lesson learned. I never made that mistake again.

The rest of my training, thankfully, was less dramatic. Day by day, the tones felt more natural, the rhythm easier to catch, the policy manuals less intimidating. And when it was finally over, I was officially released, the only supervisor fully cross-trained across law enforcement dispatch, fire dispatch, and EMD.

Ambitious? Maybe. But for me, it wasn't about titles or bragging rights. It was about knowing exactly what my people carried in every chair, in every position, so that I could carry it with them.

# CHAPTER 10

## THE DAY THE AIR CHANGED

You don't walk into a shift expecting a call to reach into your past and alter the course of your life. This day began like any other day, routine and ordinary, in the way dispatch shifts often are. Still, when I look back, I see how six minutes on the line with a call taker became the catalyst for a journey of peaks and valleys, of reckoning and self-discovery.

Dispatch trains you to brace for everything: the chaos, the silence, the call that detonates in the room, or the one that fades without resolution. Most blur together in a relentless stream of voices, addresses, and unit numbers, forgettable by necessity. If you remember them all, the weight will crush you.

But every so often, maybe only once in a career, a call refuses to be forgotten. It finds you. And in its own way, it chooses you back.

It was 2008, and I was doing a four-hour overtime shift as backup supervisor from 3 to 7 p.m. Erik was in charge that night. God, I loved working with Erik. He had this way about him, with a big laugh, larger shoes, and high-platform soles, which he proudly displayed as he sashayed across the room. His personality filled the space long before his voice did, and sometimes, out of nowhere, he'd burst into song to lighten the mood.

The evening shift beat with its usual rhythm, busy but steady, the room breathing in sync with the calls. I'd been a supervisor long enough to read the floor like a seismograph: the clicking of keyboards, the rise and fall of dispatcher voices, the subtle pitch shift that signaled something was about to go wrong. The air always shifted first, charged and invisible, like the moment before lightning.

I didn't realize it at the time, but before that shift ended, the atmosphere in that room would change forever.

Heather over at C18 transferred a missing person report to North Port, a young mother who'd left her children behind and vanished without a trace. I remember pausing, hand hovering over the keyboard, thinking how strange it was. What would make a woman walk out on her kids like that? I shook it off and moved on.

We'd had plenty of odd calls before, stories that started strangely and ended quietly. I tucked it away, not realizing this one would come back to haunt me later.

A little while had passed, then Kathy at C17 turned to me. "Kris, can you jump on this call with me?" Her voice was tight. So, I plugged in to listen to her call.

I first noticed when I started listening was, a rush of sound hit me, wind, thick and forceful, like a window cracked open in a car on the interstate. Music blared in the background. A male voice barked curses. And then, beneath it all, a woman's voice.

It wasn't frantic. It was careful. Deliberate. She repeated our questions back like they were hers, as if she were performing for the man beside her.

"Help me," she whispered.

Kathy's questions were mechanical and urgent. "What's the address?"

107

"Please help me," the woman said, the plea folded into the roar.

Kathy: "What's the address that you're at?"

The woman's voice trembled. "Where are we going?"

Male voice: "I'm not…"

She sobbed, "Please let me go."

Kathy pressed, "Hello? Ma'am? What's your name?"

"My name is Denise. I'm married to a beautiful husband. I just want to see my kids again." Her words landed like a hand pressed to my chest.

She was answering him cautiously, careful not to reveal too much. My mind was racing, running through scenarios, trying to piece together what didn't yet make sense. The man kept pressing her about a phone, and she kept insisting she didn't know. I could hear the wind whipping through the line, faint static from what sounded like the North Port tower. Maybe I-75… maybe not. No location. No signal trail. Nothing solid to hold on to, just instinct, and the uneasy feeling that something was very, very wrong.

"Are you blindfolded?" Kathy asked.

"I don't have your phone. Please, God, I don't have it," Denise breathed.

"Do you know this guy?" Kathy asked.

"No. I don't, please." Her voice cracked. "Please, God, protect me."

I told Kathy to ask what Denise's last name is. Kathy asked, "What is your last name?"

Denise answered in a whisper. "Lee"

I asked another call taker to check the recent Bolo out of North Port, remembering the missing woman from earlier, "Check North Port, missing woman, what's her name?"

She typed fast, looked at me, and said, "Denise Lee."

The room went still. I couldn't breathe. Denise Amber Lee. Alive. On our line.

My hands moved before I thought. I picked up the admin line and called North Port PD. "This is Sarasota Dispatch. We have Denise Lee on a 911 call. She's been kidnapped. She says she doesn't know who took her."

Kathy tried again, low and steady. "Can you tell what street you're on?"

"No," Denise whispered.

Then the man's voice: "Give me the phone."

Denise: "Are you going to let me out now?"

Male voice: "As soon as I get the phone."

Denise sobbed, "Help me." Silence swallowed the line.

Kathy's voice, flat and small: "Kris, He hung up."

We stared at each other, frozen for a beat. Then, action. Like a starting gun for a race. We jumped into action. We called back, but it went straight to voicemail. The signal was dead; the phone was turned off. Just a tower hit on I-75. It was 2008. Just a name. A voice. A ghost of a location. And instinct. The floor ignited. Calls flew across the room. We ran the standard checks, registered owner, vehicle info, addresses, and associates, as permitted by policy, and pushed leads to the field. We moved fast, muscle memory. Data started stacking on screens like breadcrumbs. But nothing concrete. The search spread rapidly across the area. Our units joined the neighboring jurisdiction, with state and regional agencies assisting.

It was like a net being thrown over the entire city, every interstate exit blocked, every side street watched. Patrol cars lit up intersections like warning signs, their blue and red lights casting long shadows over pavement and panic. It was a dragnet in motion. It was a last-ditch effort to catch something no one could see. But she could've been anywhere. Trapped. Hiding, waiting for a rescue that might not come.

And then the phone rang again at the supervisor's position. It was her family. They needed to hear it, her voice. They needed confirmation that it was Denise. I couldn't send the audio file. It was too large, too clunky for the system we had. So, we improvised the only way we could. I held the phone to the speaker. And together, in that strange stillness of a room otherwise filled with movement, they listened. To her calm. To her intelligence. To the unimaginable bravery in her words. They knew. The moment they heard her speak, they knew it was her.

Then the calls started coming in, one after another, like the floodgates had opened.

A relative reported the suspect had stopped by a family home; they reported seeing a woman in the back of the car and said he picked up a shovel and a gas can.

Another relative called, sounding urgent, echoing the same details they believed to be true.

I clocked out at 7 p.m. I didn't want to leave, but I had to. But it didn't feel like I had left anything behind. I lived in North Port at the time, just off Toledo Blade near I-75. As I drove home, I passed one of the intersections I'd been staring at on the map all evening, now glowing with the red-blue haze of patrol lights, officers in every direction. It didn't feel like driving through my neighborhood. It felt like driving through the aftermath of something sacred and unfinished. When I got home, I couldn't sit still. Couldn't let my body unwind. So, we went out to dinner. My husband at the time brought his portable radio, and I clung to it like a lifeline, tuning in with half an ear while the rest of me picked at food I couldn't taste. Every static crackle sent a shiver down my chest. Every bit of dispatch traffic made me pause mid-bite. Then came the update: they had stopped the car, the *Green Camaro*. He was trying to get on the interstate. I held my breath. Waiting. Praying. Was she with him? Was this it? But the next voice crushed that hope. No Denise. Just him. Just an empty passenger seat. I had hope anyway that irrational, aching kind of hope that wells up when you *need* the ending to be different. When your gut tells you the truth, but your heart still begs to be wrong.

We drove home in silence, the kind that feels like grief even before the loss is confirmed. I climbed into bed, my body heavy, my brain on fire. It was the first moment I let myself go still. But my mind... wouldn't stop. That night, I dreamed I was the one taken. I could feel the panic in my chest, the disorientation of being in a stranger's car. The helplessness of knowing something was deeply, terribly wrong, but no one could hear me. I woke up clawing at the sheets, soaked in sweat, breath coming in shallow bursts. My heart was racing like I'd run a marathon inside my nightmare. Her voice echoed in my ears. That should've been the first clue that something inside me had cracked open and started to bleed.

In the days that followed, I buried myself in the work. The next afternoon, a detective from North Port called to follow up. He wanted to know if we'd taken a 911 call from a passerby who claimed they were following the Green Camaro, the same one Denise had been in.

I told him, "No. No way. We would've known." "We would've dispatched that immediately," I told him. I would check anyway.

Everyone in the room had been locked in that night, eyes, ears, hearts focused. Still... I had to be sure. I sat down and pulled the tapes myself. Every position. Every line. Every voice. One by one, I listened. Every ring. Every whisper. Every second of static.

And then the detective called me back. "Never mind," he said. "It came into another County."

Relief flooded through me like oxygen. And then, just as quickly, it vanished. Because what if that call had been ours? What if it could've changed something or everything? What if it could've saved her? That kind of doubt has teeth. It sinks in and never quite lets go.

And then it came. The call. The confirmation. She had been found, and she wasn't alive. Not safe. She had been buried. In a grave off Toledo Blade, just miles from where I turned to go home that night. Close enough that I would never again drive that road the same way. It would be a constant reminder of those 6 minutes.

I saw Kathy, the call-taker who had been on the line with Denise, near her console. Her shoulders were slumped. Her eyes were wide and hollow, as if the news had pulled something vital out of her. I went to the Center Manager. Asked if someone planned to tell her.

They looked at me. "It should come from you." So, I did what I had to do. I walked over. Told her I needed to speak with her in the office. Closed the door behind us. She sat across from me, searching my face for anything resembling good news.

"They found her," I said quietly.

Her eyes welled instantly. "Dead?"

I nodded. "Yes." She collapsed into tears. I sat beside her. Said nothing. Put my hand on her back. Just… stayed.

Because what words do you offer when a woman does everything she can to survive, and still the outcome is unbearable? She called. She spoke. She fought. And still, someone took her life. There's no script for that conversation, no gentle phrasing that makes it easier to swallow. You can only stand in that space, in the silence that follows, and feel the truth settle in your bones.

And for Kathy, that call would settle onto her shoulders in a way that never fully lifts. At the time, none of us understood what it would become, or how far its impact would reach. We didn't know it would ripple beyond that room, beyond that shift, reshaping our region, our county, our state, and the way 911 training would be talked about forever.

That is an unbearable amount to carry for one person. I was the supervisor on the phone with her, listening, guiding, sharing the weight as best I could. And even then, I knew, I was buffered by distance and role. I cannot imagine what it was like to be the call taker, to be the sole voice holding Denise Amber Lee on the line, knowing every word mattered, knowing help depended on what you could pull from seconds and fragments.

Some calls change systems. Some change policy. But some live inside the person who answered, and that kind of weight is carried for a lifetime.

What I didn't understand at first was why this call touched me so profoundly. I'd taken hard calls before, suicides, child drownings, and crashes. But Denise's voice didn't just haunt me; it reached into something buried much deeper.

It pulled me back to being that little girl in the backseat of my father's car, kidnapped, powerless, watching the world blur past the window, wondering if anyone was coming for me. The helplessness, the silence, the way my body froze because I didn't know what else to do, it all came flooding back in those six minutes.

That kind of fear doesn't vanish. It just hides, buried under years of professionalism and control. But that day, it came roaring back, and my body went into the only mode it knew: survival. I hyper-focused. Every sound, every word, every possibility locked into place. I thought I was doing my job, analyzing, coaching, fixing, but really, I was a frightened child trying to keep chaos from swallowing me whole.

After the call, I couldn't shut it off. The same hypervigilance that made me sharp on the console wouldn't let me rest when the headset came off. My brain replayed every second like it owed the universe a better ending. I'd stare at the ceiling for hours, chasing sleep that never came.

And when the noise wouldn't quiet, when the voices and the what ifs got too loud, I reached for alcohol. It was the only thing that could dim the static, the only way to make my mind go silent long enough to breathe. I told myself it helped me unwind. But really, it helped me disappear.

Every day I drove the same route to work, leaving my neighborhood in North Port and coasting down those familiar streets until I reached the stop sign at Toledo Blade Blvd and Cranberry Blvd. Just across the road, like a wound that never closed, stood Denise's memorial. They were tied to a signpost, the faded balloons waving back and forth, the weather-worn mementos, all quietly marking a moment that changed everything.

Some mornings, I'd sit there longer than I needed to. My car idles, my thoughts circling. I'd play the "what if" game again, what if we had done something differently, what if the call had been routed to us, what if someone had spotted the car sooner. The weight of those questions didn't fade with time; it just settled deeper, like a baggage I'd learned to carry.

Other days, I couldn't even look. I'd turn my eyes toward the other side of the street, pretending to check traffic, pretending not to notice the reminder waiting there. But denial never worked for long. The truth was always in the corner of my vision; that memorial was more than a symbol of loss; it was a mirror. A reminder of how fragile the system was, how human we all were, and because failure wasn't just something that happened out there; sometimes it happened on our watch.

Over time, I realized that the stop sign became its own kind of checkpoint for me, not just on the road, but in my heart. It was where I faced the parts of the job no one talks about. The guilt. The grief. The quiet reckoning that comes with knowing you can do everything right and still lose someone anyway.

Denise wasn't just another caller. She was a mirror. Her bravery cut straight through my armor and forced me to face the parts of myself I had spent decades burying. The child who had survived by staying quiet was still inside me. But Denise? She didn't do that; she fought.

I couldn't stay silent anymore, not as a dispatcher, not as a leader, not as a woman who had survived her own storms. But the thing about traumatic stress is this: if you don't face it, it finds its way out in unconstructive forms. I charged forward, laser-focused on fixing the system, diving headfirst into change, without realizing I hadn't healed the part of me the trauma had broken.

So, I just ignored the trauma and started where I could, in the small spaces between the chaos. Between the bursts of ringing lines and the static-laced shouts over the radio, in the rare moments of quiet, I studied. I didn't just memorize buttons or scripts. I dissected the anatomy of the job, every moving piece beneath the headset, every crack where a call could slip through.

I built a guide for call takers, not a sterile, corporate binder packed with bullet points and jargon, but a living, breathing roadmap written in my own words. A first-party kidnapping guide born from experience, not policy. It included the things no manual ever mentioned: how to hear what fear tries to hide, how to catch the clues a victim slips between sentences, how to work in the space between what's said and what's meant.

The things I learned the hard way from Denise's voice.

I didn't keep it in a drawer. I took it to the floor, put it in the hands of the very people who'd use it, and asked: *What works? What's missing? What do you wish you'd known before your first bad call?* When it was solid, I sat down one-on-one with operators, replayed scenarios, and walked them through it. *What do you hear here? What's she really telling you? What would you ask next?*

Wireless 911 was still unpredictable then, a mix of miracles and dead ends. I wanted to know every glitch and every gap. I hounded our 911 coordinator with questions, dug through obscure online forums, and combed through technical documents most people would never touch. I learned the difference between Phase 1 and Phase 2 location data, why rebidding too quickly could trick the system into providing inaccurate coordinates, and how to read those shifting dots on the map as if they were a moving target.

When I was sure I understood it, I didn't keep it to myself. I'd walk over to another console and start with, "Hey, did you know…?" Then I'd show them, right there on their own screen, step by step, so they could feel the difference between guessing and *knowing*.

When I'd exhausted the phones, I moved to radios. I asked our vendor to break it down: what happens when we patch channels, how to talk on multiple frequencies simultaneously, how to pull in state channels in a pinch, and what to do when the system buckles under too much traffic. I wanted to know where a transmission went after it left my console, how far it traveled, what obstacles could kill it, and what real silence meant in that chain.

I dug through dusty binders no one had opened in years. I clicked into system menus most people avoided for fear of "breaking something." And then I passed it on, one person at a time, console by console.

No one told me to. It wasn't in my job description. But after what happened to Denise, I couldn't sit still and wait for someone to hand me the tools. I went looking for them. Learned how to use them. And then I shared them with anyone who wanted to sharpen their tools before the next call.

It wasn't a program. It was a shift in culture, slow, quiet, grassroots. And it started with the lesson Denise had left me: *Don't wait to be told. Prepare yourself now. Prepare each other.*

It didn't begin with a promotion or a title. It began with a decision: that if I were going to survive this job, I'd make it brighter, sharper, safer, for myself and the people sitting shoulder to shoulder with me.

Looking back, I see it for what it was, the earliest flicker of a teacher's heart. A leader forming in the shadows before anyone else could name it. Not ambition. Not ego. Just a calling. Because sometimes you don't wait to be invited. Sometimes you keep showing up until the room makes space for your voice.

Eventually, someone noticed. They always do. But I wasn't doing it for recognition. I wasn't chasing applause or titles. I was chasing clarity. Preparedness. I was chasing the promise that the next time, we'd do better.

In 2010, they called my name at the APCO conference and handed me the plaque for Florida Supervisor of the Year. It should have been a pure moment of pride, a culmination of midnight study sessions, console-by-console training, and years spent tearing apart our systems to understand them inside out. And in some ways, it was. But as I smiled for the camera, all I could think about was Denise. Her voice. Her courage. Her six minutes.

The ache lived just beneath the surface, like a bruise no one else could see. And under that ache was something darker: guilt. Not the loud, crushing kind, the quiet kind that follows you everywhere, a whisper in your ear. *You did everything you could. But was it enough?*

I tried to quiet the noise in my head, the endless hum of radio static and the replay of calls that refused to fade away. To cope, I focused my energy again on something I could control: learning. I wanted to understand *everything* about 911, not just how to answer the calls but how the entire system worked.

I dedicated my time to learning about the ENP certification, *Emergency Number Professional*, a title that, on paper, sounded simple, but in reality, it was the Mount Everest of 911 education. It covered every aspect of the industry, from the laws that established it to the technology that supported it.

For years, I thought I was just doing the work, fixing systems, building training programs, making sure no one else would ever miss a call like Denise's. I thought it was me pushing forward, me holding it all together, me finding purpose in the wreckage.

It began with a small group of us, four or five dispatchers working toward the same goal, but one by one, life pulled them away. Eventually, it was just me, sitting at the supervisor's console night after night with stacks of flashcards and a highlighter, drilling acronyms into my memory: CAMA, ALI, ANI, PSAP, NG911, ESI net, i3. Each one held its own world of meaning.

I studied *how* a 911 call travels, from the moment a caller presses that last "1" on their phone to the point it appears on a dispatcher's screen. I learned about selective routers, MSAG databases, and call delivery trunks, those invisible highways that carry cries for help across counties and states. I explored Next Generation 911 architecture, fascinated by how digital systems like ESI net are replacing analog copper lines, promising faster routing, richer data, and fewer lost calls.

I memorized how GIS mapping connects to caller locations, how ALI records update in milliseconds, and how the CAD system transforms a panicked voice into action on the street. I studied the layers of legislation, FCC regulations, Wireless Phase II mandates, and the standards written by NENA and APCO, the very backbone of our profession.

I spent hours reviewing call flow diagrams, tracking the invisible path of a 911 call through CAMA trunks, IP networks, Selective Routers, and ESZ boundaries. I wanted to understand what happened behind the scenes, what failed, what succeeded, and why.

During shifts, I tested myself on public safety grade networks, redundancy, diversity routing, and the difference between legacy and NG9-1-1 systems. I learned about governance models, funding mechanisms, liability laws, and the federal oversight that influenced every decision we made inside our center, even the ones we didn't realize were connected.

There was so much to absorb: technology, policy, operations, and management, and each subject led to dozens of new questions. But it gave me something essential: clarity. It transformed my anxious energy into momentum.

For most of my life, I had mastered the art of staying small of watching from the sidelines, avoiding the spotlight, and letting others take the stage. But somewhere along the way, that quiet girl who used to shrink back started reaching for something more. It didn't happen all at once. It began in small, steady steps, the kind that test your courage when no one's watching.

The morning of the exam, I was terrified. This wasn't a quick test; it lasted hours and covered everything from network topology to state legislation, emergency service zones, and database management. I remember sitting there, fingers trembling, reading each question carefully, skipping the ones I wasn't sure about, then circling back when my nerves finally gave way to instinct.

When I hit "submit," my heart stopped.
Then the screen flashed: **PASS.**
I exhaled so deeply it felt like I'd been holding my breath for months.

After all that studying, the late nights, the flashcards, the endless coffee, I had done it. I was officially an Emergency Number Professional.

The shift threw a celebration, and even the Sheriff made an announcement. I was the first ENP in our county. It was one of the proudest moments of my career. Because it wasn't just about the letters after my name, it was proof that in a world built on chaos, I could still create something steady. Even with all the noise, I could still grow.

Looking back, I see the truth I couldn't face then: I wasn't holding everything together. I was breaking in slow motion and trying to outrun it.

For years, I told myself the long nights, the manuals, the training guides, the nonstop push to "fix the system" were signs of strength. I thought if I kept moving, kept producing, kept helping everyone else, maybe I could outwork the parts of me that were falling apart. By day, I functioned on adrenaline; by night, I drank just enough to quiet the noise in my head. I wasn't coping, I was numbing. And the more I numbed, the more I lost myself.

Back then, I didn't understand what I was really doing. I was building things for everyone but me. I poured into dispatchers, created tools, wrote training materials, and whispered "You've got this" to people who were barely standing, while I ignored the fact that I was barely standing myself.

I kept telling myself I was fine because I was still functioning. Still producing. Still showing up. That's the dangerous part about being strong for too long: you mistake survival for stability.

The truth is, I was trying to find my way through the wreckage without admitting anything was broken.

It took years, and a lot of honesty I avoided for too long, to understand that I wasn't weak, I was wounded. That I wasn't failing, I was exhausted. That my so-called strength was really just armor I never learned to take off.

And now, I can see the chapters where I drifted, where I disappeared into the work because it felt safer than sitting alone with myself. I can see how the drinking became a way to turn off the replay, how the perfectionism became a shield, how the constant doing kept me from actually feeling.

But I can also see something else: even in the mess, even in the breaking, I was trying. I was searching for direction, for meaning, for a way back to who I was before everything got heavy.

And maybe that's the real story, not the falling apart, but the clawing my way back. The slow rebuilding. The small, stubborn steps toward something better. The realization that being broken didn't mean I was done; it just meant I needed to finally find my way back to myself.

.

# CHAPTER 11

## THE INVISIBLE WITNESS

I didn't realize right away what I had become. Not just a call taker or a dispatcher. Not just a calm voice in the storm. Somewhere between the adrenaline rush of my first call and the bone-deep numbness that followed my thousandth, something changed. I became a vault, a keeper of a county's secrets, sealed tight behind an invisible door.

Most people think dispatchers or call takers just send help. They picture us like air traffic controllers for chaos, moving pieces on a board. But that's only part of it. What no one sees is that people don't just call to report emergencies. They call to be heard. They call to confess. They call when their world is collapsing and there's no one left who will pick up the phone.

And that someone was me. That someone was us.

They called in panic. In rage. In raw despair that scraped the words from their throats. And I answered, calm and steady, my name unknown, my face invisible, a stranger with unrestricted access to their most private unraveling. They didn't know me. Yet, they gave me everything.

Their voices carried grief, guilt, rage, and fear. Whether their stories were fact or fiction didn't matter. What mattered was that in that moment was it felt real. And by picking up the call, I became responsible for holding their story.

The drunk who dialed night after night just to hear another human voice.

The abuser who twisted the truth until even I had to dig to find who the real victim was buried inside his story.

The teenage girl, whispering from a locked bathroom as her stepfather pounded at the door.

The exhausted mother who called 911 not for a crime, not for violence, but because her son refused to get out of bed for school, and she had nothing left.

The older woman, forgotten by her family, called to ask if someone could check her mailbox because no one had spoken her name in days.

And Roy, the habitual caller. Drunk or sober, it didn't matter. Every day, he dialed in to cuss me out, to remind me he "paid taxes." And every day, I'd sigh, press the headset closer, and tell him, "Not today, Roy. Today is not the day."

And I listened. Always. I kept my voice steady even when theirs cracked. I sent help whenever I could, my fingers flying across the keyboard, documenting every detail, every pause, every scream, each keystroke imprinted into CAD like a permanent scar on the timeline of someone's worst day. But dispatching was never just about moving units on a map. It was about holding their stories and safeguarding their secrets.

That's the part no one sees. The headset isn't just plastic and wires; it's a covenant. An unspoken vow that says: *I will hold space for your worst moment, and I will never repeat it outside these walls.* Our oath isn't just "to serve and protect." It's to carry what can't be taken alone. Quietly. Invisibly. Permanently.

The walls of the comm center are soundproof, and so are we. Outside, the silence remains sealed. I couldn't tell you how many calls I've taken, thousands? Tens of thousands? Each one is a thread. A voice. A confession. A cry for help woven into a quilt of chaos, stitched by my own hands. Over time, the fabric grew heavy. Layer upon layer until I didn't just hear trauma; I wore it.

Sometimes, those stories spilled into the public eye. A chase. A fatal crash. A child who didn't make it. The kind of calls that light up newsrooms, then get condensed into twenty-second sound bites, spun like cotton candy for prime-time ratings. I'd sit on my couch, remote in hand, jaw tight, and whisper to no one, "*That's not what happened. That's not how she sounded. That's not what she said.*"

But I couldn't correct them. Couldn't tell the world. That was the job. That *is* the job. They trusted me not just with their safety, but with my silence. And it wasn't my story to tell. My duty wasn't just to respond. It was to absorb. To carry. To contain. I was the lifeline, not just for the public, but for law enforcement, the firefighters, the medics, the invisible thread holding the broken pieces together long enough for someone else to arrive.

And all the while, I stored the calls I couldn't forget. The voices I couldn't un-hear. The stories I never asked for but still carried. That's what being a dispatcher really is: not just answering the phone, not just sending help, but becoming the vault that holds every story no one else wants to keep. And doing it silently because that's what the job demands.

When I got home, silence was sometimes the loudest thing in the room. There were nights I walked straight to the shower and stood under scalding water, steam fogging the mirror, hoping it could rinse the voices from my skin. Each drop felt like it was trying to wash away someone else's desperation, their fear, their helplessness that had clung to me all night. A baptism by faucet, begging the stories to swirl down the drain. Sometimes it worked. Sometimes it didn't.

Other nights, I didn't even get inside. I'd park in the driveway, headlights off, keys still in the ignition, sitting in the dark for thirty minutes, an hour, unmoving, unthinking, and just breathing, trying to gather the strength to step into a house where no one knew what I had just heard. Trying to switch from holding strangers together to holding dinner conversations. Trying to remember who I was when the headset came off, and if that version of me even still existed.

At first, I came home bursting with stories. Not names, never names, but wild calls, unbelievable tales, the kind of chaos you couldn't make up. I'd sit at the dinner table still buzzing with adrenaline, eager to unload it all, the drunk who called to report himself, the teenager stuck on a roof, the naked man who tried to break into the Taco Bell drive thru. My family leaned in, wide-eyed and curious, laughing at the absurdities and nodding in awe as I described moments when it felt like I truly made a difference.

But over time, the stories changed. The adrenaline diminished. The laughter faded. The calls became heavier. And I stopped sharing. Not because I didn't trust them, but because I couldn't keep making them see what I saw in my mind. Just because I never left the chair didn't mean I didn't see it. The headset is a projector, and imagination fills in what the eye never witnesses.

And mine? It became vivid quickly.

You hear a mother screaming that her son has been shot, and your brain doesn't wait for details; it paints the scene for you. Blood smeared across the tile. Trembling hands slick with red. The gut-wrenching sound of her voice splintering as you guide her through chest compressions she can't bear to do, even though you already know he's gone.

Or the 4 a.m. call from an older man, voice trembling as he whispers that his wife died peacefully in her sleep. But he can't let go. He begs me to send someone. He pleads for help. He asks me to save what's already gone cold beside him. All I can do is stay on the line until the responders arrive, listening to him beg the universe for a miracle that isn't coming.

There isn't any training for that.

So, slowly, I grew silent. I'd sit at the table, nodding at the right moments, pushing food around my plate, smiling at their stories. But I stopped sharing my own. Because how do you explain what it's like to carry hundreds of lives in your head? How do you make someone understand what it feels like to be the last voice someone ever hears? You don't. You go silent. And the more calls I took, the more silence I brought home. Until one day, I realized I wasn't just keeping secrets for the county. I was also hiding them from the people I loved.

Inside the center, silence wasn't an option. My screen transformed into a living organism of chaos, blinking and updating, demanding. At any moment, I might be responsible for dozens of deputies scattered across the county. Or up to 10 in the city. They weren't just unit numbers and flashing icons on my CAD screen, but I never forgot: those were people. Men and women chasing suspects through backyards, breaking up domestic fights, walking into unknowns with a gun on their hip, and my voice in their ear.

On a typical shift, I might handle a dozen active incidents. Three deputies are on a domestic call, and two more are on a theft case. One is serving a restraining order, and another is doing a welfare check. Some deputies are working on crashes, noise complaints, and multiple traffic stops, while I still have six calls waiting in the queue. My fingers never stop moving. I'm constantly updating: *"En route," "On scene," "Cleared,"* and assigning the next call before they even realize they're available, maintaining a continuous triage of chaos.

There's a saying in dispatch: *"You may know where you are, and God may know where you are, but if dispatch doesn't know where you are, you and God better be on good terms."* Because if something goes wrong and I don't know where you are, help might never find you in time. That was my job: to learn, to be their overwatch, their invisible partner, their lifeline. The deputies focused on one call at a time, one scene at a time. I held the map of all of them in my head, every street, every voice, every risk that hadn't yet revealed itself. I had to be prepared to respond, know where to obtain the backup, and who to get it to. And do all of it in a split second.

Even on calm days, and there were a few, you had to stay in rhythm. Feel the pulse of the room, as if it were a living heartbeat. Lose that groove, and the job will eat you alive.

And then there were the foot pursuits, a whole different ball game.

No warning, no buildup. One second, you're typing in a license plate, routine as breathing, and the next, **bam**, the radio explodes with the sound of a deputy fleeing for his life. Garbled words torn apart by adrenaline. Breath crashing into the mic. Boots pounding against asphalt. Sirens somewhere in the distance.

No location. No details. Just chaos.

The whole room shifted instantly. My thumb pressed the button, and my voice cut clean and sharp:
"10-3 Channel 1. All units hold traffic."

Silence on the radio except for them, gasping and shouting fragments. My mind scrambled to catch anything: a street name buried in static, a cross street muttered between gulps of air, the sound of sirens screaming in the background.

Foot pursuits are like firecrackers. Fast. Unpredictable. You don't get do-overs. You don't get to pause and ask, *"Say again?"* Not when they're sprinting through backyards, not when they are chasing a suspect. Your job is to repeat *exactly* what you hear, even when it's static wrapped in fear. And hope to God you catch the one clue that gets back up to them in time.

But some calls don't just spike adrenaline; they freeze time.

Supervising one night, I remember the open mic.

At first, only grunts, scuffling, and chaos spilling into the channel. Then the deputy's voice, cutting through, raw and desperate, like a man in a fight he might not win.

"HE'S GOT MY TASER!"

The room went cold. My heart pounded against my chest.

Then another voice, sharp and steady as a blade. The sergeant.

"SHOOT HIM."

Two words. Carved into me like fire branding flesh.

It wasn't just a command; it was the narrow line between life and death, spoken into a headset. A deputy with only seconds to decide. One shot. One choice. One action that would ripple for years, through rewritten policies, lawsuits filed, and the hollow look behind his eyes when he replayed it in silence later.

And us? We were the invisible witnesses, the ones who carried the echoes without ever pulling the trigger.

But law enforcement wasn't the only fire we faced. Soon, I would learn a different kind of chaos, flames that didn't originate from guns or courtrooms but from burning homes, frantic neighbors, and desperate voices begging for help as sirens chased smoke into the night.

Fire dispatch was a whole different world. Fewer codes, simpler language, but when it flared up, it burned intensely. Most days were manageable. I'd relay fire units with a clear, steady rhythm: structure fires, medical calls, lift assists. The pace of fire calls was different, slower, heavier, until it wasn't. Brush fire season changed everything.

When the wind was strong and the ground dry, fire spread faster than we could speak. Suddenly, the rhythm broke into chaos: transferring calls to other channels, juggling mutual aid requests from three different counties, tracking who was covering which station, all while monitoring two or three radio channels at once.

During fire season, there was no room for lightness. I remember days when I couldn't leave my chair, even for a break, while brush fires ravaged multiple jurisdictions and pushed mutual aid across county lines. The radio was a barrage of sirens, wind, and strained voices. All hands, all stations, all channels, until the smoke seeped into my bones and I forgot what quiet even sounded like.

A crew was caught, flames pushing faster than their feet could run, smoke swallowing their air, radios crackling with panic. When that Mayday transmission went over the air, the comm center shifted. It wasn't just sound. It was electricity, the kind that raises every hair on your arms and freezes your lungs mid-breath.

"MAYDAY, MAYDAY, MAYDAY" came screeching over the radio. Fire was closing in on them from the brush fire.

We copied the Mayday call, then played an alert tone on all channels, calling a Mayday for those firefighters. We moved all radio traffic to other channels, provided the location, and sent pages. I was sitting there, waiting and praying. Then, after what felt like forever, the firefighters gave the "All clear."

During those moments, the room became animated. Every dispatcher fell silent, eyes fixed on screens, with no one daring to cough, let alone speak. We triggered the alert, flagged the crew, paged the supervisors, pulled the coordinates, and entered updates into the chaos. Dispatchers' voices had to be steady, even as their hands trembled just enough to rattle the headset cord.

Seconds stretched into slow motion, like rubber bands snapping taut, threatening to break. That Mayday tone, low and urgent, a guttural cry from the system itself, etched itself into my muscles; the words I sent into the fire were enough.

They made it through that night. But the sound? It never left me. Even now, in silence, it echoes in my chest.

We logged every second. Recorded every breath and carried it home like contraband no one could see. That's what people never understand. They see the chair, the headset, the blinking lights on the console. But they don't see the soul behind the screen, absorbing trauma like a sponge. They don't hear the echoes that follow you into bed at night, into your dreams, into the quiet moments you wish could just be quiet.

That's the part of dispatch the world never sees, the part that never lets you go.

I didn't merely dispatch units.

I sent *hope, we sent hope,* during *chaos, survival,* and *sorrow.*

Every call absorbed something inside me: the raw scream of a mother holding her lifeless child, the slurred confession of a drunk too lonely to hang up, the jagged breaths of a teenager whispering from a closet while someone rattled the doorknob outside. I carried all of it, their voices, their panic, their desperation, and tucked it into the drawers of my chest, locking each one tight.

At least I tried.

Because some days, no matter how hot the shower ran or how hard I scrubbed my skin raw under the spray, those drawers didn't stay closed. They rattled, spilled, and came unhinged in the dark. The voices I had tried to bury resurfaced, echoing in my ears, replaying in my dreams, and bleeding into the silence of my kitchen at midnight.

I didn't just sit behind consoles. I sat at the fragile boundary between chaos and order, between life and death. My tools weren't weapons or bandages. They were a headset, a glowing screen, and a voice I kept steady even when my heart wanted to pound out of my chest.

And that voice? It was the only link between a stranger's nightmare and the help rushing toward them. A fragile thread of trust they didn't even realize they had placed in me. They didn't know my name. They'd never see my face. Yet in that moment, I was the only lifeline they had.

And I did it all silently.

Because that's the oath.

And that's the burden.

An invisible burden, but heavy enough to bend your spine. A burden that doesn't win medals or parades but still leaves its mark in your bones.

# CHAPTER 12

## FEAR RIDING SHOTGUN

During the slow stretches on shift, we'd fill the time with chatter, the kind of conversations that stitched people together in small, temporary ways. I had acquaintances at work, friends, if you squinted, but most of them didn't last outside the center walls. My circle was small, deliberately so. I had my husband, my built-in confidant, the one person I spoke to every day without fail. Beyond that, connections were more complex. Some friendships faded naturally. Others cracked under the weight of the job. A few didn't survive my habit of disappearing into silence. I never meant to retreat, but dispatch consumed me until there was nothing left to offer. And when the tank was empty, quiet always felt safer. Solitude was familiar. It was the one rhythm I knew by heart.

Still, I tried. Megan was one of those rare connections who slipped past my guard. We bonded over softball, signing up for an adult slow-pitch league once a week. Eventually, my husband joined in, and it became our ritual: playing under the lights, laughing until our cheeks hurt, and grabbing drinks after the games. One of my favorite memories is still the day we drove her little VW Bug across the state for the Florida Law and Fire Olympics in Stuart. Somewhere along I-4, the sky split open, and rain hammered the windshield so hard the wipers gave up. Megan shouted over the downpour, "My VW is like a half-circle gliding on the road!" and we laughed so hard we were crying, clutching our stomachs, tears mixing with rain. Two dispatchers off the clock, alive in the absurdity. We didn't win a medal, but we walked away with something better: a rare, fleeting sense of belonging.

I performed well one-on-one, in small circles where conversation felt safe. But as more voices entered the room, something inside me shifted. That familiar voice, the one I'd carried since childhood, would whisper, *Be quiet. Don't say anything. You'll sound stupid. You'll say it wrong.*

So when I stepped into leadership, that voice came with me. Every meeting, every briefing, every time I had to speak in front of a group, I felt the old panic tug at my throat. I had to learn to silence that inner critic, to stop mistaking fear for intuition. It wasn't easy. Some days it felt like wrestling a ghost that knew all my weaknesses. But I kept showing up, voice shaking and all, until courage started sounding more familiar than doubt.

Belonging in friendship, however, wasn't the same as belonging in leadership. Shortly after my second marriage, I became a shift supervisor. But every time I tried to advance, I hit a ceiling. For ten years, from 2003 to 2011, I chased promotion like a moving target. I studied harder, learned the politics, and checked every box. I sat through interviews where I sometimes nailed every answer and other times my mind went blank. No matter how prepared I felt, I was never the top choice.

Each rejection cut deeper than ambition. It wasn't about the title anymore; it was about validation. I wanted someone to look me in the eye and say, *You matter. You've earned this. You belong here.* Instead, I got polite smiles, a handshake, and the exact words every time: *"Keep trying."* I became the runner-up. The almost. The just-not-this-time.

Part of me began to wonder if maybe I wasn't cut out for more. But another part knew I was already leading, not from a podium, not with a title, but in the quiet ways that mattered, lifting my people through burnout, through fear, through failure. I didn't crave recognition. I craved the opportunity to improve the system.

I remember going to a theme park with a group of girlfriends once, a trip that should have been nothing but fun. The car was full of laughter, inside jokes flying back and forth, music blaring, the kind of energy that makes the air feel alive. But I wasn't in it. I was back in my head, that small, quiet girl again, the one who always felt like she didn't belong.

I watched them joke and tease, their conversations weaving so effortlessly around each other, and I couldn't find a place to step in. Every time I thought about speaking, my throat tightened, the words dissolving before they reached my lips. By the time we arrived at the park, someone had finally noticed. "Hey, you, okay?" they asked, and I gave the same answer I always did: *"I'm fine."*

The truth was, I wasn't. I wasn't angry or sad. I was just… uncomfortable. Like there was an invisible wall between me and the group, and I didn't know how to climb over it. The longer I stayed quiet, the harder it became to break out of it. So, I just sat there, smiling faintly, watching everyone else shriek on roller coasters and crack up at silly things, while I folded further into my silence.

On the outside, I probably looked calm, maybe even aloof. On the inside, I was screaming at myself: *Say something. Just say something.* But silence had its grip on me, and I didn't know how to loosen it. So, I stayed there, present, but not really part of it.

The truth was that the spotlight never felt natural to me. I was born into a guarded world, and no matter how far I went, I could never fully escape it. I learned early how to vanish in plain sight, kind of a quiet that blends in, the kind that observes more than it speaks. When I felt exposed or uncomfortable, I'd start looking for exits, curling inward until I felt invisible again.

Silence became my safest refuge. The less I spoke, the fewer eyes noticed me. In my world, attention wasn't praise; it was pressure. Sometimes, it was even dangerous. And I wanted no part of it.

In my family, I was the quiet one. At school, I drifted to the back of the room, praying no one would call my name. Even when I tried to push myself, the old reflexes fought back. Like the semester, I signed up for a public speaking class. Every day we had to read a news article aloud, just two minutes. For most people, it was nothing. For me, it was torture. My voice cracked. My face burned. My throat squeezed shut. My hands shook so badly the paper rattled in front of me. Those two minutes stretched into eternities, and I dreaded them the way some people dread the dentist's drill.

That same knot of fear lived inside me even years later, long after I'd become a supervisor. It trailed me into every interview, every moment I stood at the front of a room, every time I dared to hope for more.

That fear never let me go. It followed me into adulthood, slipping into every interview, every meeting, every room where I had to stand up and speak for myself. When I first applied for the communications job, the opening question was the simplest on paper: *"Tell me about yourself."* But the moment it landed, my brain scattered like a deck of cards thrown into the wind. I could barely string together my own name, let alone craft an answer that sounded competent. The silence stretched, heavy and judgmental, and just like that, I shut down. Blank. Again.

Every *"No"* stung, sharp and personal, but it also lit a fire. The next day, I'd slide back into my chair, headset on, as if nothing had happened. I answered the calls. I ran the floor. I coached rookies through their first cardiac arrest, steadying their hands with my voice. I smoothed out tense exchanges between field units before they cracked wide open. The headset didn't care how I performed in an interview. The radio didn't care if my voice shook in front of a panel. Out there, in the thick of noise and urgency, I led without a title. And I did it well.

Still, the dream tugged at me. Ten years is a long time to chase something always just out of reach. After another rejection, I'd drive home, park in my driveway, and sit there in the dark, still in uniform, hands locked around the steering wheel. Sometimes I'd replay the interview word for word, dissecting every stumble, every answer that died halfway out of my mouth. Other nights, I told myself it didn't matter, that I was right where I belonged. But deep down, I knew *acceptable* wasn't enough. I wanted more.

Fear had been my shadow since childhood, but dispatch taught me something fear never counted on: I could act while afraid. I could speak through a shaking voice. I could type the call, tone the units, give updates with my heart pounding like a drum in my throat. Fear might ride shotgun, but it didn't get to grab the wheel.

Looking back, maybe that's why I never walked away from the chase. Each setback left a bruise, but it also left a challenge, a dare. I wasn't just trying to prove myself to a promotion board; I was trying to prove it to me. That I could step fully into the role I was already living in, piece by piece. So I kept showing up. One call. One shift. One interview.

But fear is sneaky. It doesn't storm the door; it slips in through the cracks, wearing a new disguise every time. By the time I sat for the manager position, I told myself I was ready. I had the years. I had the experience. I had the scars to show for it. I'd been leading from the shadows long enough to know the weight of responsibility, the rhythm of a team, the burden of decisions.

Still, the moment I stepped into that room, it was like someone pressed rewind on my life. Suddenly, I wasn't a professional with a decade of leadership under my belt. I was thirteen again, standing in front of my public speaking class, paper trembling in my hands, face burning red, voice trapped somewhere between my chest and my throat while the seconds stretched cruelly, daring me to break.

A panel member leaned forward, eyes steady. "If you disagreed with a policy but still had to convey it to your shift, how would you handle that?"

My heart knew the answer. My brain knew it, too; I'd rehearsed it endlessly. In the mirror, I was gripping the bathroom counter, and in the car, whispering it over the hum of the engine, even to my husband across the dinner table. I could say it in my sleep.

But in that chair, the words disintegrated. Static roared in my ears, drowning out the practiced lines. My tongue felt like sandpaper. Thoughts scattered like dry leaves in a gust.

Inside, I screamed at myself: *You know this! Say it!* But fear sat louder, heavier, in the seat where my confidence should've been.

"Uh… could you repeat the question?" I croaked, already feeling the slip.

They repeated it, patiently and professionally. But my footing was gone. I stitched together something weak, a flat, generic line about "supporting the agency while offering feedback through the chain of command." The kind of answer that checks a box but leaves no mark.

And I knew it. I knew it as the words left my mouth. I knew it in the silence that followed, in the polite nods across the table.

Every rejection afterward felt like a stamp pressed against my chest, heavy and permanent: *See? You're not cut out for this.*

But the truth was more complicated to name; I wasn't failing because I didn't know the answers. I was failing because I hadn't yet believed the truth about who I already was.

In 2011, when a posting went up for **Operations Supervisor**, it felt like the door I'd been circling for years had finally cracked open. I told myself, *this has to be it.* No more excuses, no more waiting for the "perfect time."

I sat down at my desk and wrote my letter of interest as if my career depended on it. I listed every credential I'd fought for: Shift Supervisor, Law Dispatcher, Fire Dispatcher, EMD, Fire QA. I even tucked in the line I was proudest of, *2010 Florida Supervisor of the Year.* I have even obtained the ENP – Emergency Number Professional designation. Each bullet point felt like armor, proof that I had earned a seat at that table. When I finally hit submit, my chest was tight, like I'd just sent a piece of myself out into the unknown.

Then came the studying. I dragged out the thick policy manual, pages worn soft at the corners from years of use and started highlighting until my vision blurred. Yellow, pink, green stripes lit up the pages like confetti, everything I thought they might ask, everything I thought I might forget under pressure. At night, I fell asleep with the book still open on the pillow beside me, its weight a reminder of what was at stake.

When the candidate list went up, I hurried to the board and scanned the names. As expected, it was a strong group. People I respected. People who deserved to be there. My gut twisted anyway. *What are you doing here?* The voice whispered. *You don't belong in this lineup. They're sharper, steadier, stronger.*

I practiced silencing those doubts. Over and over, I ran through mock interviews: in the mirror with my own reflection, in the car while traffic rolled by, even with friends drafted as pretend panel members.

One night, a friend leaned back in the chair, folded his arms, and put on his best "official panel" face.

"Tell us about yourself."

I straightened, trying to sound confident. "I've been with the Sheriff's Office for over a decade, cross-trained in law, fire, and medical dispatch."

"Stop," he cut me off, grinning. "You sound like you're reading a eulogy. Say it like you believe it."

I laughed with him, but inside I was unraveling. No matter how many times I practiced, my voice cracked. My throat tightened. I could feel the panic edging closer with each rehearsal. *You know this stuff,* I told myself. *You've lived it. You've earned it.* But when I opened my mouth, it came out shaky, like someone else was speaking through me.

As the interview drew closer, it felt like I was standing at the edge of a cliff. One leap could change everything. One stumble could send me tumbling back into the shadows where I'd been stuck before.

The morning of the interview felt like a performance I'd been rehearsing in private for months. I laid my uniform out the night before, smoothed the fabric, and gave the shirt an extra dose of starch until the collar snapped back like a salute. I wanted to look like the version of myself that didn't second-guess. I wanted to look sharp, controlled, ready.

My hair had other plans. It refused to sit where I told it to, a stubborn halo that made me run a hand through it until my fingers trembled. When I pinned my badge on, my hand shook so hard the sharp end nicked my thumb, and I flinched. It was a tiny, ridiculous pain, enough to remind me I was alive and not the composed person I'd pictured.

I arrived early. The parking lot smelled like asphalt and coffee; the dashboard under my palms held the faint ghost of last night's fast food. I sat behind the wheel and rehearsed into the steering wheel like an actor chewing stage directions. Lines I'd practiced in the mirror came out thin and brittle against the leather. My palms slicked; my breath hitched, shallow and fast. "Just walk in with courage," I told myself, as if courage were something I could button up and wear with the uniform. I didn't know where to find it.

The waiting room hummed with its own nervousness. No other applicants were waiting. Just me and the plants, as I fiddle with pens or stare at the floor. When they called my name, my legs felt like they belonged to someone else walking in front of me.

I sat down and folded my hands into my lap to hide the tremor. The panel was a bright, oval table that seemed to swallow sound. Three faces looked up: neutral, expectant, professional. One of them smiled as if forgiving me the typical human foibles of the morning.

"Tell us about yourself," the first asked.

My mind went dead, clean, white, as if someone had power-cycled the part of my brain that holds rehearsed answers. I swallowed and forced a smile that felt paper-thin.

"I… um… I've been with the agency for… several years. I've, uh…" The practiced cadence evaporated. What came out was staccato and small, little filler words where conviction should have lived. I could feel every sentence land wrong, feel the air thicken around them.

The next question landed before I'd recovered. "How do you handle conflict on your shift?"

Inside, I was furious at myself. You've done this a thousand times, I wanted to shout. You've broken up fights over nothing, coached rookies through panic, and kept the floor from collapsing when everyone else was ready to break. But out loud, I sounded like someone reading a pamphlet: "I… I try to keep the peace. Communicate."

Sweat prickled down my spine. My throat tightened every time I tried to make a point. The panel nodded politely, the kind of nod that acknowledges but doesn't mean endorsement. When the interview finally ended, I stood on legs that felt borrowed, thanked them with a voice that trembled, and walked out into the bright, ordinary morning convinced I'd flubbed it.

Waiting afterward felt like slow motion. Each day stretched the space between my heartbeat and the phone. When my boss finally answered on the third morning, I felt the steering wheel in my grip like something to hold onto.

"Did they post the results?" I asked.

"Yes. "She paused, kind and clinical. "You came in number three."

Air fled me in a single whoosh. "Damn it," I heard myself say.

Number three was close enough to wound, far sufficient to hum with every old insecurity: not good enough, not steady enough, not enough. The miles home were a litany of every falter, every stammer, every drop of sweat, playing on loop. For the first time, quitting felt like a real, heavy option: a door I could close.

But even as the doubt crowded in, something steadied me. I could name the moments at work when I'd been exactly what a room needed: clear, decisive, steady. My interview had robbed me of the words in that small room, but it hadn't taken the work I'd already done. I wiped my hands on my jeans, squared my shoulders, and kept moving forward.

I never gave up.

Somewhere along the way, I stopped trying to banish fear as if it were an intruder. Fear wasn't leaving. It had unpacked its bags and moved in. So, I learned to live with it, like an annoying neighbor who bangs on the wall but never leaves. Fear became the reminder that I cared that the stakes mattered. Stage fright didn't mean I wasn't ready; it meant I was human.

That guarded girl who once turned crimson just reading two paragraphs aloud in class. She grew into the woman who now stands before rooms across the country, her headset off, her voice steady. My hands still tremble sometimes, my stomach knots, but I speak anyway.

I wasn't just surviving the headset anymore. I was shaping the room and owning it. Standing steady in a way my younger self never would have believed possible.

# CHAPTER 13

## QUIET WARS

Just before my promotion to Operations Supervisor, sometime around the beginning of 2011, I ran headfirst into one of those unforgettable lessons in workplace politics. Not every chapter of my career was filled with blaring sirens or frantic voices on the other end of the line. Some chapters were quieter, murkier, and much more draining. They weren't about chaos outside; they were about turmoil in the breakroom. Politics. And those battles could leave scars just as deep as any call.

This wasn't the loud, obvious kind of conflict you could see coming. It was the kind that slipped through the cracks, hidden behind words like "policy" and "procedure," polite enough to make you second-guess yourself. Until one day, you realized you were waist-deep in it, wondering when the dispatch center turned into the set of a bad reality show.

The irony was, I thrived in real emergencies. Give me chaos in the form of a barricaded suspect, a multi-alarm fire, or half the radio lighting up at once, and I knew exactly how to plant my feet and take control of the room. But office politics? That was a different kind of shit show. There's no protocol card for that.

The spark that lit this particular fire wasn't dramatic. It wasn't a mishandled 911 call or a failed response. It was an operator calling in sick.

Nothing unusual, except this operator was drowning. Everyone could see it. Stress and exhaustion had hollowed her out. What she needed wasn't punishment; she needed rest, maybe even FMLA, maybe counseling. So, I did what any decent supervisor would do. I told her to take the day. I covered the hole, shifted the chart, and kept the floor running. That was leadership.

The "mistake"? I didn't pass the information in the proper order. I didn't phrase it with the right buzzwords or send it through the right email. And apparently, that was enough to earn a formal reprimand. A black mark, just as my name was on the short list for promotion. Coincidence? Or calculated? Either way, the result was the same: a blow meant to knock me out of contention.

In the middle of that absurd "discussion," the Ops Supervisor threw in a side comment that revealed what this was really about: "Have you been sitting in my chair?" "Yes, just to make phone calls." "You're not supposed to sit there."

That was the pettiness that broke me. Not the reprimand, not the paperwork, the fact that it had been reduced to a chair.

"This is fucking bullshit," I said, and walked out. Not an outburst, not an attack. Just truth, raw and plain.

The fallout came quickly. I was called into the Ops Manager's office, with the Ops Supervisor already seated, a paper spread out between them like a verdict. "We're documenting you for failure to follow procedure... for disrespect... and we're recommending mandatory therapy."

Mandatory therapy. Over a sick call. Over a chair.

I wasn't burned out, I wasn't unraveling, I was standing my

ground. But there I was, treated as though compassion was a flaw and honesty was a disorder.

I grabbed the phone and escalated the issue. That's how I found myself in the Captain's office. The entire lineup sat across from him, arms crossed, showing self-importance on their faces. The Captain flipped through the paperwork, his jaw tightening with each page. Then he looked up, eyes sharp.

"If Kris is getting written up for this," he said, "then so is everyone else at this table. Because I wasn't notified either."

The room fell silent. Their backpedaling was quick and messy. Excuses tangled together until they tripped over each other. The Captain finally slammed his hand down, the crack echoing off the walls. "Enough. This petty shit about who sits in what chair and whether someone said a bad word? I can't believe I'm wasting my time on this."

In the end, no one was written up. The pile of papers sat idle, robbed of its impact. Relief flooded over me, but the ache remained.

That day taught me a lesson I'd never forget: the real threats in a comm center aren't always the emergencies that come through the phones or radios. Sometimes, the danger is internal, the kind that sneaks in quietly, poisons culture, breeds distrust and turns colleagues into opponents.

I learned that politics doesn't need a siren to do damage. It feeds on ego, on power plays disguised as "procedure." And if you're not careful, it can choke a center faster than long hours or low pay ever could.

The reprimand faded, but the lesson remained. It wasn't about policy or a chair; it was about ego. Once you see how ego destroys a team, you'll never view leadership, or silence about it, the same way again.

The thing about politics in a dispatch center is that it sticks. It doesn't wash off with the end of a shift. It clings to the walls, to the air, to the way people look at each other across the room. You can feel it in the silence when you walk in, the hush that isn't relief but tension, conversations cut short, glances exchanged, the subtle calculations about who's in favor and who isn't this week. It's like humidity: invisible but suffocating all the same.

Supervisor styles magnify it. A strong supervisor can anchor a room, giving people the confidence to do their jobs without second-guessing. But a bad supervisor? Their style seeps into everything. If they lead by fear, their people start shrinking back, too scared to decide without permission. If they play favorites, cliques form, whispers multiply, and suddenly, teamwork is replaced by territory. If they lead with ego, every call and every decision becomes a stage for performance instead of an opportunity to serve the caller.

I saw it over and over. Dispatchers who were sharp, compassionate, and steady would start second-guessing themselves after a few weeks under the wrong supervisor. They stopped speaking up in briefings, stopped volunteering for more complex assignments, and stopped trusting their instincts. Instead of growing, they shrank. Because in a toxic environment, growth isn't rewarded, compliance is.

The worst part? That toxicity doesn't stay in the breakroom. It leaks onto the floor. You hear it in the hesitation of a dispatcher afraid to make a judgment call, in the edge of someone's voice when they transfer a line, in the way a shift struggles to cover each other because trust has eroded. And in a profession where seconds matter, hesitation and mistrust can cost far more than morale.

That was the hardest lesson politics ever taught me: it isn't just messy meetings or unfair reprimands. It's culture. And culture dictates whether a comm center is a place where people can withstand the worst days on the job, or a place where even the good days feel unbearable.

Was God trying to teach me a lesson here, tolerance, patience, teamwork? What was He trying to show me through all of this?

I often ask myself that when I look back on the harder seasons, the ones that tested my character more than my skill. The politics, the unspoken tension, the moments when truth had to fight its way through whispers and egos. Those times when I felt alone, unheard, or judged for doing what I thought was right

Maybe He was teaching me to be still.

To hold my tongue when I wanted to defend myself.

To lead with integrity even when no one else is watching.

Maybe it was about humility, learning that not every battle deserves my energy, that silence can sometimes be stronger than shouting.

Looking back, I see it more clearly now. God wasn't punishing me; He was pruning me. Every conflict, misunderstanding, and person who rubbed me the wrong way, they were part of the shaping. He was stretching my patience, softening my pride, and teaching me that leadership isn't about being right; it's about being righteous.

I've learned that sometimes God uses the hardest people in our lives to teach us the most powerful lessons about grace, forgiveness, and how to stand firm without becoming bitter. Back then, I only saw the frustration. Now I see the refining.

So, when I think about those seasons of politics, of tension and quiet battles behind the scenes, I realize: God wasn't testing my position.

He was strengthening my purpose.

He was teaching me how to work with people, not against them.

How to listen even when I disagreed.

How to lead with both spine and heart.

And maybe that was the true lesson all along: that even in the messiest moments, He was still there, teaching me how to become the kind of leader, coworker, and person He could trust with more.

# CHAPTER 14

## THE WEIGHT OF THE TITLE

I made it; I was finally promoted in October 2011, a goal I had been working toward for over a decade. The promotion didn't just come with a title; it went with the culmination of years of learning the job inside and out, surviving long shifts, weathering the politics, and proving I could carry the weight without breaking. Stepping into the role of Night Shift Supervisor in 2011, the air in the center felt different the moment I walked in. Nights had always carried their own kind of weight; the phones seemed sharper, the silences longer, the crises stranger. The center felt bigger somehow; the hum of radios and computer screens was louder, and the faces of the team turned toward me with an expectation I had never felt before. I wasn't just sliding into a chair at a console anymore. I was the one expected to keep the shift steady, to make the hard calls, to notice when someone was slipping and pull them back. I was responsible for the operators taking the flood of 911 calls, the dispatchers juggling radios and units, and the supervisors working under me who now looked to me for direction. It wasn't just about *my* performance anymore; it was about theirs, too. The success of the night, and the weight of its failures, now rested squarely on my shoulders.

So along with the promotion came a new office, and an office "chair." Not the ergonomic kind, but the kind that already carried a history. Guess who I shared that office with? You guessed it: the same Operations Supervisor who, just six months earlier, had tried to slap paperwork on me over petty nonsense.

Walking into that room could have been awkward or hostile. But I chose before I ever touched the doorknob: no grudges. No carrying the weight of old battles into this new season. So, I walked in with an open mind, sat down in my new chair, and every day, without fail, I made sure to say hello. A simple word, but it set the tone.

I wasn't there to dig up old fights. I wasn't there to prove who was right. I was there to lead. And sometimes leadership isn't about grand speeches or dramatic changes, it's about the small, steady actions that show people who you are. For me, it started with respect, even when it wasn't always returned.

Being promoted didn't come with a manual. No one handed me a playbook that said, *"Here's how to lead operators, dispatchers, and supervisors when the world is falling apart at 2 a.m."* There wasn't a neat binder of flowcharts to show what to do when an officer is screaming for backup on one channel, a second dispatcher is locked in a spiral of tears after a gut-wrenching call, and the phone lines won't stop ringing. There was no laminated guide hanging on the wall to tell me how to juggle three people begging for a break at the same time, when the floor was already stretched too thin.

What I had instead was what I'd earned the hard way: long nights at the console, scars from calls that carved themselves into my memory, and the quiet lessons that came from being pushed past exhaustion and still answering the line. I had the muscle memory of survival, knowing when to speak and when to stay silent, when to let someone work through their own storm and when to pull them out of it. I had the perspective of watching other supervisors succeed and stumble, storing away their choices like unspoken training material. Most of all, I had a deep, almost stubborn belief that if I wanted this team to follow me, I had to show them I wasn't just wearing the title, I had lived the weight of it.

146

I knew if I wanted this team to trust me, I couldn't come in swinging my new title around like a hammer. Respect wasn't automatic; it had to be earned. So, I told myself, over and over again: *learn first, listen first, respect the rhythms already in place before you earn the right to shift them.* Every shift had its own heartbeat, its own tempo, and barging in without hearing it first would only make me look out of touch.

I remember giving myself the same internal pep talk before walking the floor: *Don't bulldoze. Don't posture. Don't try to be the loudest voice in the room.* Dispatchers can smell arrogance a mile away, and if they think you're faking it, they'll shut you out. Leadership, I realized, wasn't about proving I knew more; it was about proving I cared more. It meant showing up, checking in on people before the calls piled up, remembering who had a sick child at home or who had just buried a parent, and carrying those details as if they mattered, because they did. It was about being steady enough that when the storm hit at 2 a.m., they didn't just trust me with decisions; they trusted me with *them.*

That's when I leaned on the philosophy that stuck with me for years: **Geese vs. Buffalo.**

Buffalo ran headlong into a storm. They lower their heads, muscle forward, and charge straight through as if speed alone can beat the weather. It looks brave from the outside, but the reality is brutal; they scatter, each one fending for itself, battered and alone in the chaos.

Geese, though? They don't fight the storm that way. They fly in formation, a sharp "V" cutting through the sky. When the leader at the point grows tired, another quietly takes its place. They honk encouragement from the back of the line, not to make noise, but to remind the front that they're not flying alone. Their strength isn't in charging blindly; it's in knowing that survival depends on unity. The journey isn't about one bird: it's about all of them making it together.

That's what I wanted for my team. I didn't want individual heroes charging off in every direction, burning themselves out, or leaving the rest behind. I wanted us to move as one, covering for each other when the weight got too heavy, rotating leadership when fatigue set in, speaking encouragement out loud when the silence in the room grew too thick. I wanted us to be geese, not buffalo. To carry the storm together.

Of course, not every lesson came wrapped in inspiration. Some came with conflict.

Accountability mattered to me. Good or bad, it needed to be acknowledged and documented. Have you ever heard the phrase, *"But did you document it?"* That question echoes in every workplace, but in dispatch, it carries weight. Because when you went back into someone's file looking for a pattern, a string of complaints, a repeated behavior, and found nothing? It was like chasing smoke.

Documentation wasn't about punishment. It was a cycle: discuss the issue, document it, correct it, and move on. Simple in theory. Crucial in practice. But in dispatch, it was one of the hardest things to make stick.

This was something I was trying to change. Not to come down on anyone, but to stop the cycle. If there were patterns among operators, was it really a performance problem, or was it a training gap? Was it a policy that wasn't working for us in practice? Without a record to look back on, we couldn't see the larger picture. We couldn't track the patterns that would have shown us what needed to be fixed.

The pace of the center never slowed down long enough for people to stop and take notes. Shifts blurred. Supervisors were stretched thin. And sometimes the silence on paper didn't match the reality on the floor. This meant that problems repeated, complaints recirculated, and the same conversations had to be had again and again. Without the record, accountability slipped through the cracks.

It taught me something: in dispatch, people will always talk about the call, the chaos, the adrenaline. But the unglamorous part, the documenting, the paper trail, that's where real change either happens or dies.

One night, a group of dispatchers snapped a picture of another operator who had dozed off at the console. They passed it around like a trophy, snickering in the shadows, whispering behind their headsets. By the time it landed on my desk, I knew this wasn't just about one dispatcher falling asleep. This was about a team deciding whether to protect each other or tear each other down.

Before I acted, I went to the Center Manager. I told her what I'd seen, what I'd heard, and how I planned to handle it. She guided me through it, reminding me that leadership was about setting expectations, not just enforcing rules. With her support, I contacted them.

I didn't raise my voice. I didn't throw policy at them. I said what I believed to be true:

"This job will break you down if we let it. We don't need enemies inside this room; we've already got enough outside. If you see your teammate struggling, don't grab your phone. Grab their call. Tap their shoulder. Nudge them awake. Protect them the way you'd want to be protected."

The message was clear, maybe even eye-opening. But it didn't land that way. They didn't like me pointing it out. They didn't like me holding a mirror up to their choices. And instead of shifting, they pushed back.

A complaint was filed. Internal Affairs launched an investigation, not just into me, but also into the Center Manager. For weeks, I lived under that cloud, knowing that even though I had acted with guidance and good intentions, I was now under scrutiny.

The conclusion finally came back: no wrongdoing.

On paper, I was cleared. But it didn't feel like a victory.

Something in the room had shifted, subtle, but unmistakable. The energy that once felt like family now felt fractured, tense, as if a quiet current ran beneath the surface that I hadn't noticed before.

I realized then that being *in charge* wasn't just about managing chaos on the radio or holding steady when the world outside was unraveling. It was also about weathering the quieter storms, the ones that brew in the corners of the room, in whispers, in glances.

And honestly? I felt like I was failing.

What I had worked toward for years, that leadership seat I'd chased and earned, suddenly felt heavier than I imagined. I was gun-shy for a while, wounded even, trying to rebuild my footing in a space that no longer felt like home.

After that, things were never quite the same.
I became the *"them"*, the one on the other side of the table, the one they watched instead of leaned on.

It gets lonely at the top, they say. And they're right.

So, I learned to stay in the background for a while, still leading, still showing up, but quieter now. Watching. Listening. Trying to figure out how to lead without losing myself in the silence that followed.

Life on the night shift just blended in like normal after that. Once the Internal Affairs cloud lifted, the room returned to its usual hum, with radios chirping, phones ringing, and keyboards clattering in sync with the city's heartbeat. Months slipped by without any real issue bubbling up, the kind of months that all start to look the same when you're living in the fluorescent glow of 6 p.m. to 6 a.m.

Nights have their own rhythm. You measure time not by the clock on the wall but by the ebb and flow of calls. Midnight brought the DUIs and bar fights, loud music complaints spilling in like clockwork. At two in the morning, the city became strange, with oddball calls, a naked guy running down the street, and arguments in parking lots over nothing. By three or four, the room grew heavy, with eyelids drooping and bodies sagging into chairs as the adrenaline faded and fatigue crept in. Then came the dead quiet of pre-dawn, a silence so thick that every ring of the 911 line felt like an alarm.

For months, that rhythm carried us. Shift after shift, we kept our formation, flying through storms together when they hit and coasting when the skies cleared. The drama of the photo incident faded into the background, replaced by the steady grind of night shift life, the kind where you start to forget what day it is, but you never forget the sound of a radio squelch at 3:17 a.m.

# CHAPTER 15

## STARTING OVER, OUT LOUD

During the time I was assigned to the night shift in 2011-2013, my mom moved in with me. Her health had started failing, and liver failure was slowly stealing her strength. By day, I was a caregiver, juggling doctor visits, medication schedules, and the quiet, heavy moments of watching someone you love fade in front of you. By night, I was a supervisor, walking into the dispatch center and slipping back into the role of calm authority while the weight of home pressed hard on my chest.

Balancing both worlds was exhausting. Some mornings I would drive home from a twelve-hour shift, the glow of sunrise hitting the windshield, only to walk straight into caregiving mode without ever closing my eyes. The fatigue was bone-deep, but family comes first, at least that's what I believed. Having my mom live with us, though, created ripples I didn't fully see coming.

I do believe it caused a rift in my marriage. I thought stepping up for family in times of need was what we were supposed to do. I thought sacrifice would be understood, even appreciated. Instead, tension settled into the house. Resentment grew in the silences, in the unspoken words, in the space between what I thought marriage was supposed to look like and what it really was. I told myself we were still a family, that love was enough to hold it all together. But deep down, I would soon find out that we weren't the happy family I wanted us to be.

One night, we had a blowout fight, one I'm sure had everything to do with my mom living with us. He was drunk, which I might add he didn't do often, angrier than I'd ever seen him. He screamed in my face that he hated me, his voice so loud it shook something profound inside. Then, in a flash of rage, he ripped off his wedding ring and hurled it across the living room. The sound of it hitting the wall felt like something breaking inside me. I'd never seen that kind of fury in him before, and for the first time, I was scared. I don't think he even remembers that night, the words, the violence in his voice, or how small and helpless it made me feel. My mom, who was already frail and ill, and I grabbed our things, climbed into her car, and drove to her house in Englewood. I don't know if it was the alcohol or deeper resentment surfacing, but that night marked a turning point. It was the beginning of the end, the moment I realized that our marriage was slipping beyond repair. But I ignored these signs, hoping no matter what, we would make it.

The reason my mom moved in with me was simple, though heartbreaking. She and my stepfather were separated after years of his abuse. He had crossed too many lines, and by then, even she couldn't pretend it was survivable. However, the separation came with a peculiar arrangement; he still covered all of her living expenses, medical bills, and health insurance. On the surface, it looked like support. Underneath, I would later learn it was about control.

While my mom was slowly dying of liver failure, climbing the transplant list one agonizing step at a time, my stepfather was engaged to another woman. Engaged, while his wife lay hooked up to monitors, waiting for the call that might save her life. The sicker she got, the higher she climbed on the list. By January 2017, she was at the top.

I'll never forget that night, January 3, 2013. I was at work when the call came, her seventh and final call for a transplant. They instructed us to go to the center immediately. I had never driven so fast in my life.

My hands clenched the wheel, my heart pounding, praying over and over that I would make it in time. I pulled into the hospital with just five minutes to spare before they wheeled her into the twelve-hour surgery.

Kelly and I sat in the waiting room, the hours stretching out like years. We clung to each other, to vending machine coffee, to updates that never seemed to come fast enough. Finally, the surgeon came out, the operation was a success, though not without terrifying moments. Twice during the marathon procedure, my mom had gone into cardiac arrest. Twice, they brought her back.

She spent three days in the ICU before she opened her eyes. And when she did, her recovery was nothing short of astonishing. The new liver kicked into overdrive, flushing the toxins from her body, pulling the excess fluid out, giving her skin color again, giving us hope again. We watched a dying woman come back to life.

The bitter truth came later. My stepfather broke off his engagement with the other woman after my mom survived. Because survival meant he couldn't escape. If she had died, he would have been free, free to marry again, free to keep all he had built without splitting it in divorce. But she lived. And living meant he was trapped in the very marriage he had been trying to outlive.

It was a cruel reality to face that the man who vowed to love her had been waiting for her to die because it was easier than giving her half of everything.

My mom made an incredible recovery after leaving the hospital and was soon able to move back out on her own. Although she and my stepfather still kept their distance, her progress was nothing short of remarkable.

Then came the start of my divorce in October 2013. At first, I couldn't believe it. I thought it was just another fight, one of those storms we'd weathered before and come out stronger from. I kept waiting for the apology, the uneasy laugh, the silent truce that always followed. But when it finally sank in, the truth hit me hard. This time, it was different. This time, it was over.

As I look back at my life, I see we were slowly becoming more like roommates than partners, coexisting in the same space but living entirely separate lives. The routine was clockwork: come home, sleep, wake up, go to work, repeat. Days blurred into weeks, and before long, the spark that once pulled us together had dulled into quiet familiarity.

I supported him through everything: his promotion goals, his new assignments, and his dream of joining K9. I remember the day he brought the new K9 home, excitement lighting up his face like a kid on Christmas morning. The dog was beautiful, loyal, protective… but not toward me. No matter how many treats or kind words I offered, that dog never warmed up. It was almost symbolic, really, the growing distance between us wrapped in fur and teeth.

I supported him in his goal to become a sergeant, cheering him on through exams and late nights studying policies and procedures. His life at the department became his world. And I was a part of it, but never fully *in* it. Still, I aimed to be his biggest supporter, his sounding board, his home base.

I wasn't perfect, not even close. Lord knows I had my faults, too. But for so long, we were a team. We told each other everything, our secrets, our fears, the hard stuff no one else knew. There were long talks after shifts, drives with the windows down, quiet nights watching TV with the dogs at our feet.

We built a life together, or at least what we thought life was supposed to look like. Vacations to see his parents in Ohio, once even driving through a blizzard in a Mustang that fishtailed across the icy highway. Laughter, frustration, and memories frozen in the rearview mirror.

There were good moments, too, moments you believe will last forever. Like the day we renewed our vows on the baseball diamond at Tropicana Field, surrounded by the familiar blue and white of our favorite team, the Tampa Bay Rays. The smell of popcorn and fresh-cut grass, the sound of our laughter echoing across the stands, it felt like a promise that we had made it through the complex parts and that we were unshakable.

Most of my adult life was spent with a man I truly believed I would grow old with. Fourteen years. Birthdays, anniversaries, late-night talks, shared dreams. A lifetime, really.

But somewhere along the way, something changed. Maybe it was the job. Perhaps it was the silence that grew between us. Maybe it was both of us evolving in ways we couldn't explain.

I still don't know exactly where it went wrong. Only that one day, I looked around the life we'd built, and realized it no longer felt like home.

I was crushed, the kind that steals your appetite, your sleep, your focus, the kind that wraps itself around your chest and won't let go. Food lost its flavor. Nights dragged on without rest. Even work, the one place I could always bury my pain, offered no escape. I'd sit in the glow of my office, pretending to care about payroll sheets and schedules while my mind replayed everything I had just lost.

Ironically, I thought I was doing everything right. I stopped drinking, started running again, lifting weights, and cooking healthy meals, trying to reclaim the woman I was before the years wore me down. I lost fifty pounds. I was strong again. Healthy again. Whole again, or at least, I was getting there. I put myself back together, piece by piece, to the version of me he first fell in love with.

So why wasn't that enough?

When we got married, I wasn't sure if it was love in the fairy-tale sense. But somewhere along the way, between the late-night talks and the quiet Sunday mornings, I began loving him. Fourteen years is a lifetime when you've survived as much as we did together, chaos, rebuilding, and the small victories that made it all feel worthwhile.

So, when he left, I wasn't just mourning a marriage. I was mourning my best friend. The person who had seen every version of me, the broken one, the rebuilding one, the woman who kept trying even when she was running on empty. We had endured so many storms together, and I truly believed we'd get through this one as well.

But he walked away without a storm. No screaming, no final blowout. Just silence.

And silence, I've learned, can be more painful than any argument ever could.

To this day, I still don't understand why. Maybe I never will. But I know this: the pain of that loss changed me. It stripped me bare, forcing me to face myself without the armor of a title, a relationship, or a reason to keep pretending everything was fine.

It was the start of a reckoning I didn't want, but one I had to face.

Months later, after trying and failing to live under the same roof during the divorce, I packed up and got my own apartment. That move felt like the final blow. The silence in those four walls was deafening. I cried at work, I cried in that apartment, I cried until I didn't think I had any tears left. Other women, coworkers, and friends circled me, trying to hold me up when I couldn't hold myself. I tried to be strong, I tried to wear the mask of resilience, but I wasn't doing a perfect job; inside, I was broken. I was nothing of the sort.

That's when I met Robin. Thank God for Robin.

She entered my life like a breath of fresh air after years of holding it in. We were both standing amid the wreckage of what we thought our lives would be, recently divorced, raising teenagers, trying to redefine ourselves one long day at a time. She understood things I didn't have to explain. She also worked at the Sheriff's Office, which meant she got it, the hours, the emotional hangovers, the exhaustion that lingered long after the headset was off. From the start, we were kindred spirits.

We started small, coffee after shifts, texts about work drama, casual conversations that gradually became lifelines. But before long, she was the person I could call when everything felt too heavy. Dinner after work would turn into hours of talking, a bottle of wine between us, laughter, and tears weaving through the same night. Sometimes we'd just sit in her living room until midnight, the TV quietly playing in the background, unraveling the knots of our lives, marriage, heartbreak, parenting, and the invisible weight of being strong for everyone else.

Having an adult friend like Robin was a unique experience. She wasn't family, nor did I have to be "on" for her. With her, I could just *be*. I didn't need to explain the silence after a hard shift or the sudden tears that came out of nowhere. She never judged it. She'd hand me a tissue, pour another glass, and say, "You're allowed to fall apart sometimes."

We made plans, too, simple, silly, necessary things: walking loops around Henderson Park, getting lost in conversation. A masquerade party where, for one night, we could both be anyone but ourselves. Weekend brunch. Night out on the town. Those little escapes became our way of remembering that life existed outside of work and heartbreak.

Robin became my sounding board, my safe space, my "person." The one I could call when I couldn't stop crying. The one who would listen without fixing, love without judging. When I didn't know how to take care of myself, she quietly did it for me, showing up with takeout, cleaning up the kitchen, and sitting through the silence. She reminded me that even in the middle of chaos, I wasn't alone.

And it wasn't one-sided. She leaned on me, too. We balanced each other, two women walking through the ashes of what we'd lost, holding each other up when one of us stumbled. There was no competition, no drama, no pretending. Just steady, honest friendship.

Looking back, I realize that having Robin in my life was one of the first times I truly felt *safe* with another woman. Not guarded. Not performing. Just real. She helped me remember what trust felt like and what laughter sounded like when it came from the belly instead of the mask.

It wasn't about fixing each other's lives; it was about witnessing them, steadfast, genuine, unshaken, while we both figured out how to build new ones.

It wasn't easy for me at work. But when Captain Slapp arrived, the air in the center shifted. He wasn't universally liked. His ideas were big, sweeping, and unapologetic, and they didn't always land gently. But for me, in that season of my life, he was exactly what I needed.

By then, my personal life was crumbling. Fourteen years of marriage were unraveling in a slow, jagged tear that touched every corner of my world. Home didn't feel like home anymore. Some mornings, the weight of it kept me pinned to the mattress, staring at the ceiling, bargaining with myself to put my feet on the floor. On weekends, I'd stay under the covers with the blinds drawn, shutting out the daylight, numbing the ache with alcohol until sleep finally claimed me.

On paper, I was functioning. I showed up for my shifts. I wore the supervisor title. I walked the floor like I was steady. But inside, I was unraveling, piece by piece, just trying to hold the line long enough so that no one else would notice how much I was breaking.

And that's when his presence mattered. Captain Slapp had a way of demanding more, not in a cruel way, but in a way that pulled you out of your own head. His vision was forward, focused, alive with possibility, and it forced me to look beyond my own wreckage. For the first time in months, I found myself leaning into something other than grief.

On the day in April 2014 when the divorce papers were signed, it felt like walking into a courtroom made of glass, brittle, sharp, every sound echoing too loudly in my ears. Even my own breathing seemed jagged, like it didn't belong to me. My sister, Carol, was at my side, her arm brushing mine in quiet solidarity, the only thing keeping me from splintering right there before it even began.

My ex-husband had asked if we could walk in together as if proximity would make the end gentler, as if walking side by side could disguise the fact that we had been fractured for years. I told him, No. There are doors you don't walk through together once you've already shut them in your heart.

The judge's voice was flat, mechanical, a recitation of phrases that should have meant something but didn't. Fourteen years, **nearly half my adult life**, reduced to a handful of legal sentences, a shuffle of papers, and the dull thud of a gavel. No acknowledgment of the nights we laughed, the fights we survived, the family we tried to build. No ceremony for the ending, just a cold stamp that said, *Done.*

When I stepped into the hallway, he was there. Hands shoved in his pockets, shoulders hunched, eyes rimmed red. Tears cut tracks down his face. When he looked up, there was this expression, almost accusing, like I was the one who had blindsided him. Like I had stolen something from him, when in truth he had been the one to walk away. It twisted a knife in me, but not enough to make me stay. I didn't owe him my pity.

I turned and walked, my heels striking the tile with a rhythm that was both too loud and not loud enough. Carol kept pace beside me, silent but steady, the way only a sister can be when words aren't enough. By the time we reached the parking lot, the weight of it all hit me like a body blow. My legs buckled. I didn't crumble gracefully; I collapsed, raw, ugly, broken. My daughters were there, and in a cruel reversal, it was their hands catching me, their voices low and urgent: *Breathe, Mom. Just breathe.*

And there, in their arms, I felt myself age decades in a single afternoon. Not because I had lost him, the man who had already checked out of our marriage long before this day, but because I had lost the version of myself who still believed we could survive anything. That illusion died with the sound of that gavel. And with it, so did the woman who thought she'd never stand in that courtroom.

Starting over after the divorce was the hardest thing I've ever had to do. There's no guide for rebuilding a life that's been connected with someone else for fourteen years. One day, you are part of a couple, and the next, you're looking at your reflection in an empty apartment, wondering how to start over.

I had to do everything alone, pay bills, set up the electric, haul groceries up the stairs, cook for one, and fall asleep in a bed that suddenly felt too big. Every task served as a reminder that the safety net

I once thought I had no longer existed. I was a mix of sadness, anger, fear, and confusion. Mostly, I was lonely.

The first few weeks in my new apartment felt like living underwater. The silence was dense, echoing in unexpected ways. I filled it with music, sometimes country, sometimes old 90s ballads, and rode my bike around the neighborhood to feel movement, to remind myself I was still here. When I came home, my dogs, Jada and Kea, were waiting. They were my anchors. They seemed to sense that something inside me had broken. They'd curl up close at night, pressing against me as if they could keep me from drifting too far away.

Some evenings, I found myself standing at the sliding glass door, staring at the parking lot lights reflected on wet pavement, wondering if the hollowness in my chest would ever fade. I went to bed early most nights, not because I was tired, but because sleep was the only way to escape the ache of being awake.

It felt like breaking a habit I'd carried for over a decade. I didn't know how to stand on my own two feet, but I was forced to learn. Weekends were the hardest. Couples filled grocery aisles and restaurant patios, and I'd feel like an outsider looking in on a world I no longer belonged to. I didn't have a circle of friends to lean on yet, just me, the dogs, and many long, quiet hours.

But it wasn't all solitude. My sisters were my lifeline. Kelly would invite me over, and we'd stay up late with glasses of wine, laughing and crying about everything and nothing. We spent New Year's Eve together that year, me in borrowed heels, trying to feel like I still belonged somewhere. My other sister, Carol, called often, checking in and reminding me that I wasn't as alone as I thought.

Then came the unexpected acts of kindness: Jeff and Jerry, with Jerry's wife Chris, made sure I had somewhere to go on weekends. Melissa and Theresa invited me to their family Thanksgiving so I wouldn't be alone. I'll never forget that simple act, reminding me that connection still exists, even in the ruins.

That season of my life was about learning to depend on myself for the first time. I learned to see life through a new lens, not just as a means to survive, but as an opportunity to rebuild. I stumbled a lot. I cried in the parking lots of grocery stores. I had long, silent conversations with God in the car. I started therapy, sitting in a small office once a week, unpacking my anger, grief, and confusion.

And somewhere in all that solitude, I came to understand that something deeper was taking place.

I was learning self-reliance, not the kind that comes from pride, but from necessity. I had to learn it then because I would need it later: when I changed careers, when I started traveling alone, when I found love again. This season was preparing me for the woman I was becoming. I needed to fix myself, and for once, I had to do it without leaning on anyone else. For the first time in my life, I was solely responsible for myself, and this was my moment to step up.

Some days, I'd leave therapy feeling lighter. Other days, I'd sit in my car afterward and cry, realizing just how tangled everything inside me had become. But I kept showing up. Kept riding my bike. Kept walking with Robin. Kept trying to make sense of the mess.

Because that's what starting over truly involves, it's not about a single act of courage. It's about a thousand tiny ones. It's paying bills when you'd rather hide. It's grocery shopping for one. It's choosing to get up, even when your heart feels too heavy to lift.

I didn't realize it at the time, but that season was silently teaching me something sacred:
I wasn't just learning to live alone.
I was learning to live as myself.

CHAPTER 16

WHERE PAIN BECAME A LESSON PLAN

While I was handling my divorce personally, a position in the Training Department opened. Captain Slapp and the rest of the Command Staff were in the middle of implementing significant changes to Communications. And if you ask me, they weren't just changes, they were much-needed lifelines. If we kept pushing forward with the old mentality of *"That's how we've always done it,"* we were bound to sink. The job was evolving, the calls were getting more complex, and our people needed tools, not just tradition.

The door cracked open at just the right moment. And I knew, almost instantly, this was it, the role I'd been waiting for. Looking back at my history, the signs were all there. I'd spent years mentoring on the floor, steadying rookies as their hands shook on the console, walking new hires through their first tough nights, showing them the shortcuts that saved seconds when seconds mattered most. I wasn't just surviving the job; I was teaching parts of it all along.

Stepping into Training felt less like a promotion and more like a calling, one I didn't even know I'd been preparing for. And honestly? I needed it.

I was clearly in a place where I needed a distraction from my personal life, drained by grief, loss, and the kind of heartbreak that doesn't leave bruises but still takes your breath away. At work, I wore a headset. At home, I faced silence. The kind of silence that weighed on your chest and echoed inside the walls. I was quietly drowning, trying to pretend I wasn't.

So when the chance to move into Training arose, it felt like a lifeline, a rope thrown into deep water. I grabbed it with both hands. I needed something to pull me forward, something to remind me that I was still capable of building, shaping, and leading, even when everything else in my world was falling apart.

Mark Twain once wrote, *"The two most important days in your life are the day you are born, and the day you find out why."*

For most of my career, I believed my "why" was simple: to answer the call. To be the voice in the dark, the calm amid chaos, the one who stayed steady when everyone else fell apart. However, as the years went on, that purpose started to change. It didn't happen all at once; it gradually crept in, somewhere between exhaustion and awakening.

I still remember the day of the interview. It wasn't like any other I'd had before. This time, I carried myself differently. I wasn't the same timid dispatcher hoping to prove I belonged. I had scars now, proof that I'd survived the storms. I walked into that room with my shoulders squared, my head up, and my voice steady. I spoke with the kind of conviction that comes only from knowing what it costs to stay standing.

When I walked out, I didn't just *hope* I had the position; I *knew* I did. For the first time in a long while, I felt a flicker of certainty inside me.

A week later, it was official: I was now overseeing Training, soon renamed the Professional Development Section. The responsibility was heavy, the workload relentless, but I welcomed it. Because, more than anything, it felt like a *purpose*. A new chapter. A reason to get up in the morning when everything else in my life still felt unsteady.

When Captain Slapp asked me to move into the training section, I didn't realize I was stepping into the second most important day of my life, the day I started to understand *why* I had survived so much.

Until that moment, dispatch was about endurance: show up, stay sharp, keep everyone safe. But standing at the front of that training room for the first time, with a row of new faces staring back at me, I felt something different stir inside, something that tugged at my heart instead of draining it.

This wasn't just about teaching procedures or software. It was about *people*. It was about preparing new dispatchers for the same storms I had barely survived myself. It was about helping them build armor that could protect them without turning them to stone.

I remember standing behind a trainee's chair one afternoon as she handled her first real 911 call. Her voice trembled, not from fear, but from the weight of knowing that someone's life was hanging on her words. I wanted to reach out, steady her shoulders, and whisper: *You've got this. Breathe. You were made for this.*

And in that moment, I realized, God had been preparing me for this all along. Every heartbreak, every sleepless night, every shift that nearly broke me, none of it had been wasted. It was being repurposed.

This was my why: to build others, to strengthen what once broke me, and to turn the pain I carried into tools that could help someone else survive theirs.

The headset was my battlefield.

Training became my calling.

That was the day I fully embraced my purpose, not the kind that shouts, but the kind that quietly transforms lives.

Don't get me wrong, I was still wounded. Still healing and still taking one day at a time. But this work gave my pain somewhere to go.

When I moved into Professional Development in October 2013, my days were busy from dawn to well past sunset. Mornings started with new-hire orientations, wide-eyed recruits clutching notepads, nerves buzzing through the room. I'd guide them through the basics: how to log in, how to breathe through the panic, how to find their voice when a caller's world was falling apart.

By afternoon, I was running scenario drills, including in-progress burglaries, missing persons exercises, and mass-casualty scenarios that mirrored the chaos they'd soon face through their headsets. I paced the front of the classroom, voice calm, movements deliberate, answering every question with the steadiness of someone who had lived it.

On the outside, I appeared composed, professional, confident, and in control. Inside, my chest sometimes felt like it was caving in.

Some days, Captain Slapp would drop another project on my desk, rewrite the field training checklist, rebuild the EMD refresher, or overhaul a policy that hadn't been touched since 1998. I never said no. I took it all on, buried myself in it, and stayed late long after the lights dimmed in the center.

It wasn't just dedication. It was survival.

The hum of voices from the dispatch floor, the chatter of operators switching shifts, and the faint static from radios through the walls made it easier to face than the silence waiting behind my front door.

So, I stayed. I worked. I built.

And slowly, piece by piece, I began to heal.

At home, the silence was suffocating. It wasn't the kind of silence that brought peace; it was the kind that pressed against your skin, heavy and unrelenting. The apartment walls felt too thin, as if they

166

couldn't contain the grief inside them. Every creak in the floorboards, every hum of the refrigerator, every passing car outside seemed to echo the same truth: I was alone. The air itself felt hollow, and the space seemed colder after sunset.

At work, I felt purposeful. I knew who I was when the headset was on. But at home, I experienced grief, raw and formless, spilling into every corner of the night. So, I did the only thing I knew how to do: I chose work. I threw myself into it with every ounce of energy I had left, not just to excel but to stay upright, to outrun the memories waiting for me in the silence. Every policy I rewrote, every training module I built, and every late night spent under the buzz of fluorescent lights, all of it all became my way of preventing myself from unraveling completely.

That was around the time my youngest daughter moved back in with me. She was sixteen, beautiful and defiant, with fire in her eyes and a restlessness I recognized all too well. Things at her father's house had started to spiral, the kind of teenage chaos that sneaks in quietly until it suddenly gets out of control. She was hanging around the wrong influences, making impulsive choices that threatened to derail everything she had worked for.

She had so much potential, a sharp mind, and a natural athletic ability, giving her a real shot at a softball scholarship if she stayed focused. I couldn't stand by and watch her future slip away, not knowing what losing direction could cost. So, we packed her things and moved her in with me.

It wasn't smooth. Not at all. She hadn't lived full-time with me since she was little, when bedtime stories and bubble baths still made everything better. Now she's a teenager. She's strong-willed, independent, and carries an attitude that makes every talk feel like a standoff. She doesn't want to leave her friends, routines, or her sense of freedom. To her, moving in with me felt like a punishment. To me, it was a rescue.

The transition was bumpy. Doors slammed, rattling picture frames. Heated arguments went past midnight, with both of us too stubborn to yield. Tense car rides where silence was louder than words. But between the storms, there were small victories: a solid game under the field lights, a teacher's report that made my heart swell with pride, and a rare, quiet evening when we actually laughed over dinner, that kind of laughter that reminded me that beneath all the defiance, she was still my girl.

I had to relearn how to parent her. Raising a sixteen-year-old wasn't like caring for the little girl I remembered, the one who used to fall asleep on my shoulder after softball practice. This version of motherhood required balance, knowing when to tighten the reins and when to loosen them. I had to remind myself that discipline wasn't the same as distance, that control wasn't love. She didn't need a warden; she needed a steady presence, someone who would show up no matter how hard she pushed me away.

It wasn't perfect, but we found our rhythm. Slowly, almost imperceptibly, we started rebuilding what time and circumstances had torn apart. We learned how to share space again, trust each other, and live under one roof without feeling like strangers. She grew up before my eyes, and in many ways, I grew up again alongside her.

That period also brought unexpected closure from another part of my life. Her father and I, after years of silence and resentment, started having honest conversations. Genuine ones. Long talks when the kids weren't around, when there was no audience and no need to defend our old mistakes. For the first time, we faced the past without flinching.

He spoke first. His voice was quieter than I remembered, less defensive, more deliberate. He talked about our marriage, how young we'd been, how lost, how we had mistaken chaos for passion and stubbornness for strength. Then came the apology. Not the casual kind people give to tidy up the past, but the heavy, measured kind that comes from years of reflection.

He admitted that his temper had been a monster he couldn't control at the time. He had his own trauma to overcome. That he hadn't known how to love without trying to dominate, and that his immaturity and anger had left scars he could never fully undo. His voice cracked when he said, "I know what I did. And I'm sorry."

Hearing that from him, the same man who had once caused me so much pain, felt surreal. For a moment, I was unsure what to do with it. Part of me wanted to shut down and dismiss it as too little, too late. But another part of me, the older and gentler part, just sat there and listened. Because the truth was, I needed to hear it.

We were kids back then, trying to raise kids of our own. Too young to realize that love isn't enough if you haven't learned to conquer your own demons. Talking it through didn't erase the history between us, but it gave me something I hadn't known I was still searching for: peace. The kind that settles quietly, not like a revelation, but like a relief.

And for him, maybe it was redemption, a chance to face the wreckage and name it for what it was.

But there were nights, long, restless nights, when it didn't feel like purpose at all. It felt like punishment.

Either way, it was good to finally say it out loud, to acknowledge what was, what we had survived, and the truth that we had both grown since then. There was something freeing in that conversation, like setting down a box you didn't realize you'd been carrying for years. It didn't erase the past, but it softened its edges. For the first time, I could breathe in the same room with those memories without feeling like they were swallowing me whole.

That night, as I sat in the stillness of my apartment, I said the only words I knew how to say:

*"Lord, I trust the doors You close and the ones You open. Even when it feels like loss, help me believe You're leading me somewhere I can't see yet."*

It wasn't a polished prayer, not one you'd see framed in a church hallway. It was raw, whispered through tears, my voice breaking as I spoke. But it was honest. I was holding onto faith like a person clings to a ledge, not out of certainty, but out of a desperate need to survive the climb.

I was still sifting through the wreckage of my life when Captain Slapp started sending us to conferences, sessions meant to expand our

169

understanding of online learning, adult education, and new training technologies. They should have felt like a break, a chance to recharge and step away from the grind of the center. But even in hotel rooms hundreds of miles from home, the silence followed me.

I remember sitting in those neatly arranged rooms, with the hum of the air conditioner as the only sound. My suitcase was half-open on the floor, and my phone glowed faintly on the nightstand, unread messages, unanswered texts, conversations that had gone quiet long before I ever boarded the plane. I scrolled through them, anyway, rereading the same silences and replaying the same goodbyes. The distance between me and the life I lost stretched across every mile.

When the dust finally settled, and the moves, heartbreak, and long nights of pretending I was fine had all evened out, there was no dramatic rebirth waiting for me. No reinvention. Just the steady, familiar rhythm of work. The headset. The policies. The endless stream of projects that never seemed to stop multiplying. They became the rope I held onto when everything else inside me felt like it was unraveling.

And in the middle of all that stood Captain Slapp.

His leadership didn't coddle, but it didn't crush either. He had this uncanny ability to hand you something heavy and make you believe you were built to carry it. He challenged me in ways that stretched me without breaking me. Where others saw a job title, he saw a person still capable of more.

Some days, he'd lean against my office doorframe, arms crossed, coffee in hand, and ask, "How's it going?" The question was simple, but his tone always carried weight, like he actually wanted to know the answer, not just fill the air. On other days, he'd drop a thick folder on my desk, his expression unreadable except for the faint smirk tugging at the corner of his mouth. "You've got this," he'd say.

And the crazy part was, I believed him. Even when I didn't believe in myself, I believed *him*.

Our conversations went far beyond the daily grind of staffing charts and scheduling headaches. We analyzed policies line by line until the margins were filled with red ink. We examined the call-handling guide as if it were a puzzle that could always be improved. We debated state certification requirements, argued over what the academy curriculum should include, and spent hours reimagining what true preparedness meant for a dispatcher.

We delved into the mechanics of online learning, how to reach people not just behind screens but behind emotional walls. We discussed what it truly means to prepare someone for a call that could shatter their world in six minutes or less. Sometimes, he'd lean back in his chair, sigh, and let me present my case. Especially when I argued that *emotional survival* should be taught alongside CAD commands.

Other times, our discussions would turn into full-blown debates, sharp, passionate, and exhausting. There were days when one of us would walk out mid-sentence just to cool off, slamming a door on the way to get air. But it always stayed behind closed doors. Out on the floor, we stood united, one front, one message. The staff never saw the friction; they only saw the cohesion.

One night, we argued intensely about staffing. He wanted to pull someone from 911 to handle the radios. I stood my ground. "You see boots on the ground," I told him, voice steady but firm. "I see the voices we'll miss if no one answers."

He didn't give me the win that night. He never did, not outright. But later, he circled back, casual, almost playful, with a wry grin, and said, "You may think you're right, but I'm *always* Right."

Then we both laughed, the tension dissolving as quickly as it had built. That was his way of keeping things human, never letting the work overshadow the respect beneath it.

Another time, he tried to lower hiring standards to get people in the door faster, desperate to fill empty chairs. I told him no, flat out. "You can't cut the standards and expect to get quality people through the door," I said, my tone unflinching.

He pushed back strongly, his logic steady and pragmatic. We argued back and forth for days, exchanging points across desks and via email until, finally, he made the decision. He won that round, but not without listening to me. He *always* listened. Even when we disagreed, he never dismissed me.

Those battles, late-night debates, and moments when my voice shook but didn't break, shaped me. They pushed me to define what I believed, not just follow orders. They taught me to stand up for my perspective, even when it wasn't popular.

And somewhere in the middle of all that, in the mess of policies, passion, and purpose, I found something I hadn't felt in a long time: my voice.

Not just as a supervisor.
Not just as a trainer.
But as a leader.

From 2013 to 2017, we built something that became the heartbeat of the center, a training program that outlasted every shift, storm, and personality that passed through those doors. Step by step, policy by policy, checklist by checklist, we assembled it like a foundation poured layer by layer with steady precision.

The Captain and I spent countless hours beneath the hum of fluorescent lights, surrounded by binders stacked like bricks and whiteboards covered with scribbles of ideas and deadlines. There were days when the office smelled of burnt coffee and dry-erase markers, nights when the hallways outside were silent but our conversations still filled the room.

The training office built everything from scratch, scenarios, manuals, refreshers, and documentation, each piece inspired by lessons we learned the hard way. We wanted our new hires to have the tools we never had. No more guessing their way through their first calls. No more being thrown into the fire without water. Now, they have resources: detailed checklists, hands-on simulations, and mentors who stand behind them not to judge but to guide.

172

For the veterans, those who had weathered a thousand midnights and carried invisible scars beneath their uniforms, we built something for them, too. Refresher courses that reignited their confidence. Workshops that sharpened their instincts. Quiet reminders that their experience still mattered, that they hadn't been forgotten in the push for "new." We wanted them to know that growth wasn't reserved for rookies; that even after decades behind the headset, they could still evolve and still find purpose.

It was never just about teaching procedures. Anyone could memorize ten-codes or follow a CAD sequence, but that wasn't training; it was just repetition. What we were really creating was belief.

We wanted dispatchers to *feel* the weight of their role, understanding that their words could be the line between chaos and calm, life and death. Our goal wasn't just to make them competent; it was to make them confident. We wanted them to hear the truth in their own voices, trust their instincts, and truly believe they had the power to make a difference.

And somewhere amidst all of that, as we rebuilt the department from the ground up, I started rebuilding myself. Every lesson I shared about resilience, every exercise on control under pressure, and every message about finding your calm in chaos were also messages to me. I was teaching myself how to heal while pretending I was just doing my job.

But the reality of dispatch and leadership is that no matter how much you grow, you're never free from scrutiny. No one is. Pride doesn't make you bulletproof, and progress doesn't render you invisible. Every action, call, and decision is recorded, time-stamped, and replayed. There's no erasing a bad day or quiet failures.

Behind the headset, everything lives forever, every second logged, every hesitation heard, every word weighed by someone who wasn't in the chair when it happened. Supervisors listen. Coworkers whisper. Managers evaluate. And the public waits, quick to judge the one mistake they'll never understand.

The higher you climb, the narrower your margin for error becomes. The light that once guided your progress now shines too brightly. And as I learned firsthand, leadership doesn't elevate you above scrutiny; it places you directly under it.

Still, even under that pressure, I held my ground because what we were building was bigger than me. It was worth every critique, sleepless night, and whispered opinion. It proved that even in a world that measures you by your mistakes, you can still create something lasting and meaningful.

# CHAPTER 17

## UNDER THE HEADSET, UNDER THE MICROSCOPE

In a 911 center, judgment is constant. It doesn't just come from your supervisors; it comes from every angle: coworkers' side-eyeing you from across the room, the public second-guessing your every word, the media ready to pounce on mistakes, and even other centers who are more than happy to critique from the sidelines. And in those, the off comment *"Why do you ask so many questions?"* From the moment a caller dials those three numbers to the moment the line disconnects, every second is captured. Every breath you take, every pause you let hang in the air, every word you choose, it's all part of the record. And all of it can, and will, be replayed.

*Did you answer fast enough?*

*Did you ask the right questions, in the exact order, at the exact time?*

*Did you sound calm enough? Empathetic enough? Professional enough?*

QA reviews were like pop quizzes from hell. You never really knew when you'd get pulled into the little room, your call queued up like an exhibit at trial. I hated it every single time. The first time I heard my own voice through those speakers, I cringed. Dispatchers all share the same first thought: *Oh God, do I really sound like that? I sound like a walkie-talkie swallowed a chipmunk.*

Still, as much as I dreaded them, those reviews had a purpose. They caught mistakes. They taught us lessons. And sometimes, they burned a memory into your brain so deep you never forgot it. For me, that mundane call was *the call that felt like a dumpster fire.*

And yes, I mean that literally.

I was still relatively new, still in that "hey, I'm actually getting the hang of this" stage, when I got summoned for a QA sit-down. My stomach dropped. The supervisor gave me a polite smile and slid the protocol cards across the desk. That smile said everything: *Brace yourself, kid. This is gonna sting a little.*

She hit play.

*Ring… ring…*

"911, what is the location of your emergency?" my voice echoed, higher pitched than I remembered, a little robotic, the kind of tone you only hear when you're trying too hard to sound calm.

"Umm, hi," the caller said. "I'm not sure if this is an emergency, but I think the dumpster behind the TJ Maxx is on fire."

At the time, the call felt easy. No screaming. No chaos. Just a concerned citizen reporting a flaming garbage bin. But playback has a way of stripping away your confidence.

"Okay, what's the address of the TJ Maxx?" I asked.

She hesitated. "I'm not sure. I'm just parked in the lot."

"You see the fire, right? "

So, I did what we all do. I became part dispatcher, part detective. I pulled up the map, cross-referenced it, and hunted down

176

the address. So far, so good. Then I grabbed the fire protocol card and jumped right in.

Or so I thought.

The supervisor paused the playback. "Read the scripted question out loud," she said.

I glanced down at the card. The words on the card and the words I had actually said weren't even close cousins. I asked a leading question, improvised, "made it sound better" in my head. And in the process, I'd skipped over a key piece of information.

I groaned, loud, long, full body. "Ughhhhh. My bad. I'll do better next time."

We both laughed, because honestly, what else can you do? It wasn't a catastrophic error. No one was hurt. The dumpster was extinguished, and the trash never stood a chance. But the lesson landed. Hard.

Even a *dumpster fire* deserves protocol done right.

In the moment I learned that shortcuts have no place in dispatch, even on the calls that seem small, the ones that tempt you to roll your eyes. Because at the end of the day, the job doesn't care if it's a burning house or a burning trash can. The expectation is the same: precision, professionalism, and doing it right the first time.

Outside the safety of the dispatch center, the world isn't always kind. Public perception? It can be brutal. All it takes is one recording, one sliver of a call ripped from the chaos, stripped of context, and aired on the evening news, and suddenly the dispatcher becomes the villain.

*"Why didn't she ask the right question?"*

*"Why did it take him so long to act?"*

*"Why didn't he sound more urgent?"*

*"Why do you ask so many questions?"*

The media loves a headline. They'll take a ten-second clip and loop it endlessly, pairing it with ominous background music and dramatic narration. And then they'll unleash the armchair experts, people who have never sat in the chair, never held a life in their headset, to tear apart every syllable. To them, it's entertainment. To us, it's a career, a calling, and sometimes, a wound that never heals.

What the public doesn't see is the other side of that call. Most don't realize we're following a structured script designed to pull out the most critical details in the shortest time possible. It's not robotic, it's precision under pressure. They also don't hear the suicidal caller on Line 2, whispering through tears, while Line 3 flashes with a cardiac arrest. They don't know that the dispatcher has already worked four consecutive 12-hour shifts because three people called out sick, and someone must keep the lines open. They don't feel the fatigue gnawing at your body, the kind that no amount of caffeine can fix. They don't see the invisible math, triaging chaos in your head while trying to sound calm and unshaken on the line.

And then came Denise Lee's call.

That one changed everything. It didn't just ripple through our center; it shifted an entire industry. Overnight, it became *the* call: studied in classrooms, played in training rooms, discussed at conferences across the country. Haunting. Unrelenting. Every time it's played, the pause button follows, and the commentary begins.

"She said hello too many times."
"She sounded uncertain."
"She didn't take control fast enough."

The truth is, that call was closely examined by the public, by professionals, and by dispatchers themselves. But when a moment becomes a case study, it's easy to forget there was a person behind that voice, a trained professional operating under extraordinary pressure, making decisions in real time without the benefit of hindsight.

Here's what has always mattered to me: when the operator realized she needed assistance, she asked for it. That's what we're trained to do when a situation becomes complex or unclear. She reached out, and she worked as part of a team. That matters.

It's easy to dissect a call when you already know the ending. We now see timelines, transcripts, and headlines that weren't available in the moment. She didn't have that view. She was living it second by second, trying to make sense of fragments, to build order from chaos.

Those of us who've sat in that chair understand the difference between classroom analysis and lived experience. It's one thing to study a call with pause buttons, hindsight, and emotional distance. It's another to be the one with the headset pressed to your ear, adrenaline spiking, trying to find the right words in the middle of uncertainty.

I don't speak about it with anger; I speak about it with conviction. Because behind every recording that becomes a teaching tool, there's a person who bore that weight in real time. And that truth deserves compassion as much as critique.

That, to me, is courage.

It's what I tell every operator I've ever supervised:

Don't sit in silence. Don't stay stuck.

If the call feels too big, if your gut tells you something's off, ask for help. Call me. Get a supervisor on the line. We'll walk through it together. That lifeline between the operator and the supervisor isn't just policy; it's trust. It's knowing you're not alone in the fire.

Yet the aftermath was brutal. Public scrutiny was relentless, and even within the profession, judgment came fast. The event became a symbol, but the human being inside the headset was often forgotten.

That kind of weight can break even the strongest dispatcher if we're not careful, if we don't change how we train, debrief, and treat each other afterward.

Critique will always be part of this work; feedback is how we grow. But so should grace, especially when someone has the courage to say, "I need help."

That is not a weakness.

That is survival.

And it's the kind of strength this profession should honor, not punish.

At the Sheriff's Office, there is a Quality Assurance program. And let me be clear: it wasn't about armchair quarterbacking or playing "gotcha." That was and is never the point. But not everyone saw it that way.

Some operators felt picked on. They'd walk out of a review session muttering under their breath, venting to anyone who would listen about how the feedback was too harsh, too picky, too relentless. And honestly? I understood it. No one likes having their work picked apart, especially in a job where the margin for error is razor-thin and the pressure never lets up. You pour everything you've got into a call, and then someone sits you down and points out the one detail you missed, the one script you paraphrased, the one pause that lasted a second too long. It stings.

But the goal of QA was never to tear anyone down. It was to protect the standard. To make sure the person on the other end of the line, the caller whose world was falling apart, got the best of us. Not just the fastest answer or the loudest voice, but the clearest, safest response. QA was about safety. About clarity. About doing no harm while doing the hardest job in the world.

And I'll stand by this: it's necessary. Without those guardrails, without those bumpers in the lane, we don't grow. We don't sharpen. If you don't correct the small stuff, it's only a matter of time before it snowballs into the kind of mistake that ends up splashed across the news or, worse, costs a life. I'd rather walk out of a review with a bruised ego than carry the weight of knowing my mistake destroyed a family.

Eventually, I joined the QA team myself. I took on oversight of the Medical, Fire, and Law Enforcement QA programs, which meant I wasn't just on the receiving end anymore; I was the one pressing play. I was the one hitting pause. I was the one asking the hard questions: *Did they follow protocol? Did they give the units what they needed? Did they buy the caller one more minute of survival?*

It gave me a front-row seat to what operators were really up against. And let me tell you, most of them, even the ones who complained the loudest about QA, brought so much heart to the headset. They wanted to do better. They wanted to get it right. They just needed someone willing to push them past "good enough."

Lori, the woman who actually sat and listened to those calls' day in and day out, had one of the most challenging jobs in the building. Her desk wasn't covered in flashing lights or ringing phones, but in its own way, it carried just as much weight. Every week, she'd pull calls at random, never knowing what she was about to step into. Sometimes it was a textbook-perfect response, smooth and steady. Other times, it was a slow-motion train wreck you could hear unraveling second by second. Most of the time, it was something in between.

She'd put on her headset, press play, and listen. Really listen. She analyzed tone, pace, word choice, and every detail against rigid protocols that didn't care about the human on the other end of the line. The scoring sheet never accounted for the dispatcher being on hour eleven of a twelve-hour shift, or the fact that their last caller had been a mother performing CPR on her toddler. The system didn't grade on a curve. It was black and white: did you ask the exact question in the exact order, or didn't you?

Then came the most challenging part of her job: delivering feedback. Eight hours a day, five days a week, Lori sat across from call takers and dispatchers, replaying their work back to them like a mirror they didn't always want to look into. Sometimes she got to celebrate with them: *"This was solid, right down the line. Well done."* Other times, she had to pause, rewind, and point out the places where fatigue, nerves, or bad habits had crept in. But the difference with Lori was how she did it. She never talked down. She never made it personal. She knew the

181

human being across the table was usually tired, stressed, and already harder on themselves than she ever could be.

It wasn't glamorous work. There were no parades, no medals, no news stories celebrating her diligence. But it was essential. Lori had the rare vantage point of hearing the whole spectrum, the calls that read like someone was following a script word for word (because they were), the ones that spun out of control as panic or confusion took over, and the rare ones that felt like art.

Those were the ones that gave her hope and gave the rest of us a standard worth chasing. The calls were where a dispatcher's timing, instincts, and tone blended perfectly, where you could almost *feel* the exact moment, they built a bridge across the chaos and pulled someone back to safety.

Lori taught me something I never forgot: QA wasn't just about compliance. It was about protecting the integrity of the lifeline. In a room where perfection was expected but rarely possible, her work was the quiet, relentless push to make us just a little sharper, a little stronger, a little better than we were the shift before.

There were operators like Jen. She was a master at weaving protocol into conversation so seamlessly that you almost forgot she was using a script at all. It was like listening to music instead of a checklist. She'd open a call with, *"Okay, Charlie, tell me exactly what happened,"* and the tone in her voice carried a calm steadiness that cut straight through the chaos. You could *hear* the caller start to settle, their frantic breathing evening out as if Jen's composure gave them permission to believe they could handle this.

Then came the questions, every one of them in the correct order, exactly as required, but softened by her delivery. *"Alright, how old is she?"* she'd ask, and the caller would respond, their voice less jagged, their words less tangled. Jen never sounded rushed. Never sounded cold. She hit every mark on the card and still managed to sound like she was sitting right there beside them. That's what reasonable dispatch sounds like. Not robotic. Not panicked. Just steady, confident, and real.

And then there were the other calls. The mechanical ones.

You could spot them immediately: operators who asked the questions exactly as written but drained every ounce of humanity from their voices. Flat tone. No inflection. No compassion. They sounded like they were counting ceiling tiles while reading the script. Not because they didn't care, I knew they did, but because they were terrified of missing a single word. Fearful of losing points on a QA form. They were so laser-focused on technical perfection that they lost sight of the human on the other end of the line.

And that's the heartbreaking part. On the other end of that monotone voice wasn't just a call to check a box. It was a mother holding her choking toddler. A teenager whispering through tears about an abusive boyfriend in the next room, a man clutching his chest in his driveway, struggling to breathe. And when I sat down with those operators afterward, headset cords tangled on the table, playing their own voice back to them, they'd wince. They hated how they sounded. But by then, the habit had settled in like concrete. They had been so conditioned to survive the scrutiny of QA that they'd stopped hearing themselves as a lifeline.

That's when I would push back gently: *"Listen to yourself from their side. Hear what they're hearing."* It was like trying to unwind a steel cable - slow, challenging, and frustrating work. But it mattered because tone matters as much as timing.

You can follow every step of the card and still fail the one thing that matters most: making someone feel heard. And in this line of work, that single thread of connection can be the difference between panic and peace, chaos and control.

Quality Assurance was never about being perfect. It was about being better. One call at a time.

One of the most critical lessons in dispatching is that everything starts and ends with location.

Protocol, empathy, tone, multitasking, none of it matters if the address isn't correct.

Every agency phrases that first question differently. At ours, it was:

**"911, what is the location of the emergency?"**

That wording was deliberate. "Location" could mean a street, an intersection, a business, or a landmark. It gave callers options. And it carried weight.

Mid-career, I was on a shift when a call drove that truth home in the hardest possible way. A frantic parent reported a baby not breathing. The operator moved fast, entered the address, verified spelling, and launched the response. Everything looked perfect on screen. But our county had a hidden trap: duplicate street names in different municipalities. The CAD auto-populated the wrong one. The error delayed the response.

It didn't change the medical outcome, but it changed everything else: how we trained, how we verified, how we lived with the responsibility that came with one line of text.

In the aftermath, leadership rewrote the policy: every address must be confirmed with a cross street *and* a city, no exceptions. It wasn't bureaucracy; it was survival. In a county full of duplicate road names, that second question could be the difference between a rescue and regret.

Quality Assurance made address verification its first-graded item. From then on, sending help to the wrong place was no longer a clerical mistake, it was a potential tragedy.

Years later, as I was leading the Professional Development Section, I started to notice a pattern. Even our best call-takers, the ones you'd trust with anything, sometimes skipped the cross street. Not because they didn't know better, but because they *thought* they knew. They recognized the neighborhood, the subdivision, and the plaza. Familiarity bred confidence, and confidence quietly bred shortcuts.

That's when I learned the term **"Normalization of Deviance."**

It's what happens when minor rule-bending becomes routine because nothing bad has happened, yet. The shortcut works once, then twice, then always... until the day it doesn't.

Knowledge wasn't our problem; habit was. The question wasn't *"Do they know the rule?"* It was *"Have they stopped believing they need it?"*

And "yet" became the most dangerous word in the room.

We couldn't loosen the policy; too much was at stake. But endless QA penalties and retraining weren't fixing behavior; they were fueling burnout. So the answer had to be awareness, not punishment. The fix was storytelling: showing the *why* behind the rule, not just its wording.

When you attach a human cost to a checkbox, it stops being bureaucracy and starts being purpose.

That incident changed how I led. It reminded me that "routine" and "safe" are not the same thing.

In dispatch, what becomes comfortable can quietly become dangerous.

And the day we stop verifying what we *think* we know, that's the day familiarity turns fatal.

Being under a microscope, especially when it's by another dispatcher, can be brutal. There's a fine line between peer accountability and outright judgment, and let's be honest, we don't always walk it gracefully. That's where the supervisor is supposed to step in: the buffer, the translator, the one who bridges the gap between *"what just happened"* and *"what should have happened."* But in the heat of a shift, that bridge can get wobbly fast.

Communication isn't always clear when the phones won't stop ringing, radios are stacked with traffic, and the tension in the room is thick enough to choke on. A dispatcher pressed for time might skim the CAD screen, miss a detail, or enter a comment that doesn't quite match what's unfolding. And when something doesn't make sense, when the narrative doesn't line up with the screen, the room reacts.

I've heard it a thousand times:

"Who coded this?"

"What does that even mean?"

"Why would you do it that way?"

Voices rise. Frustration hangs in the air like static. And just like that, someone's shouting across the floor for clarification because there's no time to type it out. Seconds matter. One transposed digit, one wrong zone, one comment that doesn't match the facts, it can throw everything off. Units get delayed. Help ends up on the wrong side of the county. Suddenly, the call isn't just chaotic; it's compromised.

I've seen dispatchers rip each other's work apart, not because there was an actual mistake, but because it wasn't *their* way of doing things. That's not quality assurance. That's ego. And ego doesn't make the shift safer; it just makes it louder. Sure, sometimes those heated complaints uncovered a fundamental issue: a missed question, a wrong code, a note that didn't match the audio. And when that happened, we adjusted. We trained. We learned. But more often than not, the critiques led nowhere. Just bruised pride and another operator walking on eggshells, terrified to move the cursor because someone might be watching over their shoulder.

And here's the part no one likes to admit: every dispatcher I've ever worked with, even the ones burned out, even the ones clinging to the job by a thread, didn't come in planning to screw up. They were tired. Overworked. Drowning in overtime, running on caffeine and fumes. They were human. But the system still demanded perfection.

So, when people ask me what makes a good dispatcher, I don't point to QA scores or how quickly they can recite a protocol card. I don't hold up statistics, speed, or perfect phrasing like trophies.

I ask different questions:

Can they think clearly when everything goes sideways?

Can they adapt without falling apart?

Can they admit when they're in over their head and ask for help?

Because in this job, success isn't about flawless calls. Flawless doesn't exist. It's about what you do *after* the mistake. It's about recovery. It's about how fast you find your footing again, how open you are to learning, and how well you treat the people beside you, even when the headset feels like it's crushing your skull and the weight of the shift is pressing you into the chair.

That's the philosophy I wanted to carry into leadership. My job as a supervisor wasn't just about handing out write-ups or highlighting mistakes on a QA sheet. It was to create an environment where people felt safe enough to admit when they were struggling, without fear of being torn apart by their peers. I wanted to be the kind of leader who reminded the room that we were geese, not buffalo: we were in formation, flying together, taking turns carrying the weight.

If my team left a shift bruised by the calls, that was inevitable. But if they left bruised by each other? That was on me.

# CHAPTER 18

## THE QUIET YES

When I finally chose to leave the Sheriff's Office in March 2017, there was no cinematic moment to mark it. No speech or no slammed doors. It wasn't defiance or rage that carried me out; it was something quieter, heavier, a knowing that pressed into me the way silence does after a long, unrelenting storm. A whisper that had been waiting patiently all along finally rose to the surface: *It's time.*

It didn't come with fireworks or fanfare. It came with stillness. With the sense that my spirit had already moved on, and the only thing left was for my body to follow.

Looking back now, I see how God had been rearranging the pieces long before I was willing to admit it. He was nudging me toward change in ways I didn't yet recognize, closing doors I never would have had the courage to shut myself, moving people out of my orbit, shifting circumstances so subtly that I could pretend I was still in control. But I wasn't. He was making a way where I was too afraid to carve one.

I told myself I was staying out of loyalty, out of commitment, out of duty to the team, to the badge, to the mission. But the truth ran deeper and darker than that. I stayed because I was afraid of who I would be without the headset. I stayed because routine had become a crutch, and grief had disguised itself as responsibility. Staying gave me a script to read from when the silence at home felt unbearable.

The truth is, I stayed too long. God knew it, and deep down, I knew it too. But at the time, I mistook surrender for failure. Letting go felt like weakness and walking away felt like I was abandoning something sacred. What I couldn't see then, but I do now, is that surrender wasn't failure at all. It was faith. It was trust. It was finally admitting that I didn't have to carry the weight forever, because God had already been carrying me.

The signs had been there all along, but I was blind to them. Too close. Too entangled in the everyday grind, too busy extinguishing everyone else's fires to notice that my own flame was sputtering to embers. My patience was gone, evaporated by years of strain I refused to name. I snapped at things that didn't deserve more than a sigh: a training document left out of order, a classroom left messy, a database that refused to format the way I thought it should. My voice would rise over details that once would have rolled right past me. Somewhere along the way, I had stopped solving problems and started circling them, stuck in endless loops of planning and replanning long after the expiration date of my peace of mind.

I told myself the lie I'd always leaned on: if I just worked harder, pushed longer, stayed later, the meaning would return. If I poured enough of myself into the job, purpose would rise out of the ashes. But deep down, I knew better. This wasn't the purpose anymore. It was survival. And I was running on fumes.

Yet even in that exhaustion, there was pride. The Training went into overdrive. We had built something in Professional Development that was real from nothing but grit, frustration, and a stubborn refusal to let another generation walk blind. We weren't handed a polished system or a thick binder of instructions. We inherited chaos. Paper files yellowed with age, outdated protocols buried in cabinets that hadn't been opened in years, philosophies so stale they no longer matched the world we served. "This is how we've always done it" wasn't a tradition; it was a prison.

So, we tore it all down, piece by piece. We dragged the mess into the light, exposing the cracks, the gaps, and the fragile scaffolding that held everything together. We turned it upside down and poured it onto the floor like a puzzle that had never truly fit. And then, brick by brick, we rebuilt. Slowly. Intentionally. With sweat in our hands and vision in our bones.

We carved out absolute onboarding paths. Training platforms that actually worked. Systems that prepare people instead of setting them up to fail. We brought accountability into the same room as compassion and made them shake hands. We stopped reacting and started anticipating. We opened the floor for curiosity, not just compliance. We gave rookies the things we never had guidance, tools, someone checking to make sure they weren't burning alive while pretending they were fine.

We did it for them, the new ones, the ones with wide eyes and open hearts, stepping into a career that could chew them up before they had the chance to stand tall. We did it because we remembered what it felt like to be thrown into the fire with nothing but instinct and stubbornness. We did it because we refused to let silence, tradition, or fear define the next generation the way it had defined us.

And though my body was breaking, and my spirit was fraying, I held onto that truth: we built something that mattered.

The Training Team didn't just throw a binder together and call it training. We built the manuals we always wished we'd had when we started. Real manuals, not just bullet points and policy blurbs, but chapters with subsections, side-by-side comparisons of right and wrong, and scenarios pulled directly from the field. Pages that showed rookies what the job actually looked like when the headset was on and the clock was ticking, not the sanitized version someone thought looked good on paper.

And once we had the foundation, we went bigger.

We designed a full call-taking academy, structured, deliberate, and uncompromising. No more guesswork, no more "you'll figure it out." Every skill had a benchmark. Every benchmark had a test. And those tests weren't just about memorizing codes or policies; they were about performing under real-world pressure. Could you steady your voice when a caller was screaming? Could you track units when the radio traffic stacked faster than your fingers could type? That's what we measured, because that's what mattered.

From there, we built an entire curriculum. Calendars. Milestones. Progress trackers. Our training team replaced the old "shadow a trainer until they think you're ready" approach with something intentional, repeatable, and measurable. Trainees knew where they stood, trainers knew how to coach them, and the whole process had integrity.

The Training team also moved continuing education out of the penalty box. No more filler modules or death-by-PowerPoint to check a box. We launched an online platform that logged training in black and white, showing exactly who had completed what. Proof. Accountability. Clarity. And for the operators, it wasn't busywork anymore; it was a chance to sharpen skills without burning them out.

And because memory is fallible and bias is human, we created a documentation system that remembers for us. Every certification, review, commendation, and correction is logged in one place. Clear. Consistent. Professional. No more "I didn't know." No more "Well, so-and-so never had to." The excuses disappeared in the light of a system that treated everyone equally.

What we built wasn't just paperwork. It was a culture shift. A promise to the next class of dispatchers that they wouldn't be left to sink or swim the way we had been. It was our way of saying: *You matter too much for us to leave this to chance.*

Of course, it wasn't seamless, far from it. There were bumps, plenty of them. Some days it felt like we were flying a plane held together with duct tape, patching holes while turbulence rattled the cabin. But even then, we held the line. Expired certifications? Not on our watch. Sloppy records? Not acceptable. Complacency disguised as tradition. Not good enough.

The decisions weren't always popular, and we knew it. Change rarely wins applause at first. People grumbled when we tightened processes, rolled out new benchmarks, or insisted on documentation where before there had been only memory and hearsay. But we weren't chasing popularity. We were chasing progress.

And once the foundation was steady, we didn't stop. We kept asking, *What else?* What else could we build, refine, or reimagine so that no dispatcher would feel like they were walking blind into the fire? We layered new courses, refreshed curricula, experimented with technology, and continued to push until training wasn't just an afterthought; it became the backbone of the entire operation.

It wasn't about creating a perfect system. It was about making a living one, something that could adapt, stretch, and grow with the people it was designed to serve.

Under Captain Slapp's leadership, and let me tell you, that man had vision, even when it was inconvenient, we pushed harder than ever. Together, we built a law enforcement call-handling guide from scratch, created mini-training sessions, and remediation plans. These standardized procedures had never been documented, and we launched a Mentor Program that finally gave rookies something we had never had guidance from day one. We partnered with the local technical college, opened our doors to public tours, and hosted job fairs that showed people the heartbeat of our center. We updated technology that had been limping along for years and even won an award for it.

We didn't just modernize. We optimized. We reimagined what dispatch could look like when training and professionalism worked together, rather than grinding against each other.

And through it all, I absorbed everything. I was mentored. I was pushed. I was seen. Somewhere in those long nights and hard decisions, I started to see a version of myself I hadn't met before. She was still me, but steadier, more deliberate, less reactive. Not the woman who white-knuckled her way through another shift, but the leader who could rebuild the machine so the next generation wouldn't have to endure it the way we did.

As much as I wanted to hold on, I started to realize something I'd fought against for years: letting go isn't always a loss. Sometimes it's the space needed for what's next. Looking back, I wonder if this was the path all along, if God had been guiding me here with quiet, steady steps. Maybe it wasn't a shove out the door but a gentle hand leading me forward.

The truth is, I didn't want to leave. This work wasn't just a paycheck; it had become my mission, my identity, and proof that every hardship I'd endured mattered. But doors close for a reason. Not to punish us, but to protect us. Sometimes, God has to pry away what we cling to so our hands are free to receive what we would never have reached for on our own.

And behind all that progress, the truth was stark: I had to ask myself, was I wasn't healing? I had gone through a divorce that left me hollow. I was dating in a world that felt like quicksand. My youngest daughter was growing older, heading off to college, while I tried to hold it all together for both of us. On the outside, I looked polished. Professional. Productive. But on the inside, I was dodging the deepest wounds, the childhood trauma I had buried, the abuse I minimized, the grief of Denise's call that still replayed in my sleep.

I hadn't dealt with any of it. I had gotten better at functioning around it.

Until God put an opportunity in front of me that I couldn't ignore. It wasn't loud or dramatic, just steady. Clear. Unmistakable. The kind of moment that doesn't beg for attention, but changes everything if you're brave enough to say yes. And then, unexpectedly, the past came calling, not to haunt me, but to invite me into something healing.

It was January of that year (2017), just before I left the center. It wasn't the first time I had met Nathan. We had crossed paths before. I had met him at the APCO Conference, when I won the Florida APCO Supervisor of the Year award; he had also visited our agency several times over the years. On this visit to our center, he invited me to attend one of the classes he and Ryan were teaching across the country. A course built around Denise's story. Her legacy. Before the class began, we spoke privately. Nathan looked at me, gentle, steady, and gave me something I didn't even know I needed: permission. "If you want to share that you were the supervisor on duty the night Denise called," he said, "you can. And if you don't… that's okay too." He didn't push. He didn't prod. He gave me grace. Space. A moment to … be. And so, I walked into the room carrying the weight of a decade, and sat in the very back, like I always did. Small. Quiet. Trying to be invisible. Sweating under my blazer. Heart pounding. My hands wouldn't stay still. The class began with introductions that consisted only of a name and agency. Around the room it went, one by one. My turn crept closer, and I still didn't know what I would say. I didn't know if my voice would come out steady or shattered. I didn't even know if I could speak. But when it reached me, I stood up, shaking, uncertain, a lump in my throat, and said:

"Hi. I'm Kris. I'm from the Sarasota County Sheriff's Office… and I was the supervisor on duty the night Denise called 911.

And then I sat down. The room went still. Gasps. Stares. A few people leaned back, startled, stunned. Not in judgment, but like they had just felt the weight I'd been carrying press down on them, too. Like I'd thrown a rock into still water, and the ripples reached everyone. My world was spinning. My chest was tight. I felt raw, exposed, as if I had just said something I wasn't supposed to say out loud. It felt like admitting something taboo. But what I didn't expect… was what came next. Relief. Not immediate. But rising, like something inside me finally exhaled after holding its breath for years.

That day, as Nathan and Ryan stood at the front of the room, something in me released. Not all at once, slower than that. Quieter. Like the weight of years began to lift one ounce at a time, as their words settled deep into the places I had long sealed off. They weren't just teaching a class. They were offering something sacred: the truth, laid bare. And it wasn't about sensationalizing Denise's story or dragging us through the trauma again. It was about *facing* it and *naming* it, *owning* it.

Until that moment, I had always kept myself tucked behind the roles I knew best: dispatcher, trainer, supervisor. Titles that made sense. Labels that felt safe. But sitting in that room, listening to them walk through the timeline, the gaps, the missed opportunities, I saw myself in a way I hadn't before. I wasn't just someone who lived through that call. I was someone who had *never fully grieved it.* Not really. Not deeply. Not out loud.

The way they spoke, with clarity, with compassion, with purpose, invited me to see the call not just as something that haunted me, but as something that could teach. That could change people. That could *save* people. And for the first time, I was able to revisit that day not as the woman at the console, heart pounding and trying to stay composed, but as an observer. Someone with enough distance to study the moment, to examine what went wrong, and ask how we could do better. It wasn't about blame. It wasn't about guilt. It was about grace. And healing. And responsibility. Responsibility to honor the voices we couldn't save. To protect the ones still calling. And to remind every dispatcher in that room, me included, that our voices still matter. And that doing better isn't just possible. It's the only way forward.

I don't think I ended up in that class by chance. The timing was too perfect for that. I was already falling apart, questioning who I was once my armor started to slip. And then that class hit me just when I needed something to wake me up. The voices in that room, the message, the way it all came together, none of it felt random. It felt deliberate. A push I didn't realize I needed, hitting me right when I'd been stuck for way too long.

I hadn't planned on leaving the Sheriff's Office then. It wasn't even on my radar. But a few months later, a new opportunity presented itself, and everything changed. Looking back, that class was a turning point. I was meant to be in that room, hearing Nathan and Ryan, hearing the truth laid out in a way I couldn't ignore.

I'd been pushing through the days, trying to understand the weight I was carrying. But beneath all that effort, something else was already forming. A transition I didn't expect.

About a month later, the job offer came through, solid, legitimate, and clearly matching my next steps. It was from a company seeking someone who could program 911 systems, train dispatchers and administrators on the new 911 system nationwide and speak the language of the work through real experience. Someone who had built training programs from the ground up. Someone who had lived it, not just learned it.

Someone exactly like me.

The decision to leave the Sheriff's Office wasn't easy. It felt like failure, like walking away from the one place that had shaped me. But underneath the fear was something deeper, something I couldn't shake.

So I whispered the words that had been stirring in me:

*"Lord, I trust the doors You close and the ones You open. Give me the courage to walk through."*

It wasn't the first time I'd prayed it, and I wasn't sure I believed it yet. But I said it anyway.

It terrified me. Leaving Sarasota? That was no small thing. It was the place where I grew up. The center where I became who I am. The voices I trained beside. The people who knew my shorthand before I ever spoke it. Walking away felt like betrayal, like leaving family behind. But it also felt like... freedom. Freedom to start again. Freedom to heal. Freedom to follow what God had placed in front of me, even if I didn't know where it would lead.

My daughter was in college. No toxic relationship waiting at home. No scared child inside of me. No unfinished business anchoring me in place. So, I said YES.

And twenty years later, I found myself back where it all began, at Quartermaster. Only this time, I wasn't being fitted for my first uniform or nervously signing for gear I hadn't yet earned. I was turning it all back in.

One by one, I laid the pieces on the counter: the stiff polyester pants, the crisp white uniform shirts with sweat still ground into the seams, the scuffed utility belt that had dug into my hips through a thousand shifts. I handed over the badge and name tag, the small bits of metal that had once carried so much weight, both pride and burden.

It was strangely quiet. Just me, sliding across the tools of an identity I had carried for half my life.

I remembered the first day I picked them up, the way the fabric smelled new, the way I stood taller, almost believing the uniform could make me into someone stronger than I felt inside. Now, after decades of calls, chaos, and quiet sacrifices, I was giving it all back. Not because it hadn't mattered, but because it had. Because I had given it everything I had to offer.

Walking out of Quartermaster that day, my hands were empty, but my shoulders felt both lighter and heavier all at once. Lighter without the weight of the gear. Heavier with the truth that an entire chapter of my life had just closed behind me.

Handing in my badge and headset felt like peeling off a layer of skin. Dispatch had been part of my identity for so long and letting it go cut deep. But I understood this wasn't abandonment; it was release.

So, I prayed one more time:

*"Lord, I trust the doors You close and the ones You open. I choose to walk forward, even when letting go of the old chapter hurts."*

In two weeks, I would be boarding a plane to Connecticut, my first assignment in this new world. Alone. Nervous. Brave. Armed with nothing but experience, determination, and a trembling kind of faith, this was where I was meant to be. My purpose wasn't gone; it had simply taken on a new form.

I zipped up the suitcase and looked at it as if it might swallow me whole. Everything I knew, every comfort, every certainty, was left behind. Tomorrow, I'd be on the road, teaching strangers in rooms where nobody knew my name. No headset. No badge. No safety net.

Just me.

And for the first time in a long time, that was enough.

That night, I prayed for the exact words I had spoken before, but this time they carried a different weight:

*"Lord, I trust the doors You close and the ones You open. Give me the courage to walk through, and to believe I belong on the other side."*

What I didn't realize back then was that saying "yes" to that new career would change more than just my job title. Amidst layovers and late-night hotel check-ins, I met a man who would quietly, patiently become my husband.

It's funny how life works. I spent years failing in the dating scene after my divorce, pursuing stability in all the wrong places. Then, when I followed my heart in my career, I entered something uncertain but meant for me, and doors began to open in ways I never saw coming. It was as if the universe had been waiting for me to act, trust, and say "yes."

It wasn't a lightning-bolt romance. No Ah-Ha moment. No music swelling. It was quieter, slower, steadier, and real. The kind of connection you don't even register at first. Like a sunrise that takes its time. One minute, the world is dark, and the next, without warning, everything has a soft, gold edge.

One weekend at home, my youngest daughter and I were out shopping for something decent for me to wear on an upcoming date. Nothing dramatic, just me trying to look like someone who knew how to date again. While we were out, we ran into one of her old high-school friends. The girl asked what we were up to, and when my daughter said we were shopping for a date, her eyes lit up instantly.

"Oh my god, my dad's single," she said, like she'd been waiting for this exact moment.

The funny part was that we already knew each other. Years earlier, we stood on the dirty bleachers at softball games, cheering on our girls from opposite sides of the field. Back then, we were just two parents making small talk about batting orders and weather delays.

She insisted, and I mean *insisted*, that we come to her graduation party that Sunday. I did the polite nod and the "maybe," but I had no intention of showing up. Social gatherings weren't exactly my comfort zone. I was always the one who thought better of things halfway out the door.

But the two girls had already decided they were running this operation. It took them about forty-eight hours to get us both on board. She pushed him, my daughter pushed me, and suddenly a simple shopping trip had turned into a coordinated matchmaking effort.

Eventually, he and I ended up on the phone, awkward at first, both of us clearly aware we were being herded like cattle by our daughters. But he had an easy way of talking, steady and unforced. By the end of the call, he invited me to the party.

When Sunday came, I drove my daughter over, parked the car, got out, and immediately told her I wanted to go home. She gave me that teenage side-eye that basically said, *Get it together,* and nudged me forward. So, I walked in.

We weren't strangers, but we'd never seen each other in this context, no bleachers, no softball dust, no chaos. Just two adults being shoved toward each other by kids who believed we deserved more than loneliness.

And somehow, it worked.

We ended up talking the entire evening. No nerves. No weird tension. Just easy conversation that felt like we'd known each other longer than we actually had. Not forced. Not heavy. Just... comfortable.

Before the night was over, we slipped out to grab something to eat. Nothing fancy. Just two people easing into something neither of us expected.

And that's how it started, not with sparks flying, but with a quiet pull that felt steady and honest from the very beginning.

What struck me first wasn't some grand gesture. It was his steadiness, a calm that didn't demand attention but grounded everything around it. He saw me in a way no one else ever had, not as a woman white-knuckling through life, trying to hold broken pieces together, but as someone who had already survived the wreckage and was still standing.

He didn't flinch at the rough edges, the scars, the shadows I slipped into when the world got too loud. In a life where people had taken and taken, his presence did the opposite. It didn't drain. It restored.

With him, I could finally breathe. I didn't have to prove anything. I didn't have to hide the parts I used to bury under work, alcohol, or silence. I could tell him the truth, the trauma, the guilt, the moments I still struggled to forgive myself for, and he stayed. He didn't try to fix it or smooth it over. He listened. And somehow, that was enough.

It wasn't a fairy tale. It was better, it was real.

He was the kind of person who made hours pass unnoticed, with conversations shifting from lighthearted banter to the kind of truths I hadn't even spoken aloud to myself yet. And when I finally did, he didn't pull away; he leaned in closer.

That connection became another reason to keep saying yes, to the travel, to the risk, to the unfolding of a life I hadn't dared to imagine. It reminded me that even after everything I'd endured, life could still surprise me in beautiful ways.

And through it all, I could feel God's quiet hand guiding me, weaving redemption through the miles, airports, hotel rooms, and laughter. I hadn't realized it then, but He was leading me all along, not just toward a new career, but toward the kind of love that finally felt like home.

My new position kept me on the move in every way possible, as it does today. I mentioned one of my first job was in Connecticut, where I hopped from one 911 center to another, guiding dispatchers through the unfamiliar process of system cutovers, watching their lifelines shift from one console to a brand new one.

I was learning too, but at a different level. I didn't just learn the system; I lived it. Sat shoulder to shoulder with operators, explaining what was happening as the techs worked in the background, translating between two worlds:

*"This is just a test call, not live."*

*"Okay, we're transferring the 911 trunks now. You'll still get calls, just routed slightly differently…"*

Sometimes I'd catch it in their shoulders first, that rigid tension pulled tight as piano wire, and then in their eyes, fixed on the screen like nothing else existed. I remembered that feeling, remembered being in their seat, and remembered the voice on the other end of my own phone, the one who asked every night if I was eating, if I was resting, if I was okay. Even when I brushed him off, he never stopped asking.

I did two of these cutovers a week. Then I'd fly home Friday night just long enough to breathe my own air, swap out the clothes in my suitcase, and reset… only to do it all again by Monday.

Monday mornings became their own ritual: the shrill buzz of the alarm, the weight of my suitcase in my hand before coffee even hit my veins, airport parking lots under a pale sunrise. TSA Precheck was salvation, shaving minutes off serpentine lines. Boarding early, laptop opened, dropping into my seat like it was just another office chair.

And somewhere in that rhythm, his messages began to fill the spaces between flights, a simple *"Good morning "*text message before I walked into the center. *"Be safe, "*before I boarded. The kind of small, steady gestures that sneak past your defenses and remind you what it feels like to be cared for without condition.

The routine settled in and no longer required thought. Land. Follow the slow shuffle to baggage claim. Stand under fluorescent lights that feel too bright after a full travel day, waiting for a suitcase that always looks like every other one. Rental car counters blur together, key fobs, signatures, directions given too fast to matter.

By the time I pull out of the airport, I'm already switching modes. Mapping the route to the hotel. Noting landmarks without realizing it. Later, a quiet drive past the site, where to park, which door to use, and how early to arrive. It's a familiar pattern now. Nothing remarkable on its own. Just the steady rhythm of travel, preparation, and repetition that keeps the work moving forward.

Idaho. North Carolina. California. Colorado. Hawaii, Alaska, Texas, Wisconsin, Oregon, Wyoming, Arkansas, Ohio, Montana, Dominican Republic, Washington DC, Virginia, Kentucky, Alabama, Georgia, Florida, Louisiana, New Mexico, Arizona, Washington, Michigan, Illinois, Minnesota, New York, New Jersey, West Virginia, South Dakota, Idaho, Texas, Missouri, and Tennessee. Each state another dot on the map, another room full of dispatchers whose stories became part of mine.

In Greenville, NC, I noticed a dispatcher wearing a Denise Amber Lee sweatshirt. I paused. Could've let it pass. Didn't. *"I was the supervisor on duty when Denise called in,"* I told her quietly. She looked at me with a gaze that was beyond recognition, empathy, and weight. *That's why I do what I do,* I said. She didn't answer, and she didn't need to. Healing doesn't always come from words. Sometimes it comes from being seen.

In Madison, NC, a dispatcher pulled me aside and told me not to forget about the small centers. In Such centers, dispatchers live in the same neighborhoods they serve, where the job and community are inseparable. Her voice cracked as she talked about the lieutenant they lost during Hurricane Helene. About her children. Her team. Her family of dispatchers. *I see you. I hear you;* I told her. And I meant it.

Detroit, MI, gave me a recruit sitting off to the side, too quiet, too watchful, like she hadn't decided if the headset belonged to her. After training, I stopped her: *"Hold on. This job is tough, but it can be rewarding."* She nodded, thanked me, and walked away. I don't know if she made it. But sometimes all you get is a sliver of a moment to plant a seed that might grow later.

202

Monterey, CA, an administrator practically buzzing with excitement over the new features, leaning forward in her chair, energized by the possibilities.

Park, MT, a dispatcher, told me she loved her community, how she could raise her family there, and still answered the call.

Camden, NJ, is a patient, kind, resilient community that shows me that even in the hardest places, people still open themselves to learning.

And then, St. Bernard Parish, LA. The director carried herself with the quiet strength of someone who had seen hell up close. She told me about leaving the center during Hurricane Katrina, about what it felt like to walk out of a building that was supposed to be the community's lifeline, knowing she might never return. Her words carried the weight of survival, of guilt, of rebuilding from nothing. I didn't interrupt. I didn't try to fix it. I just listened. And when she was finished, all I could offer was the truth I've carried everywhere: *I see you. I hear you.*

The truth is, over almost nine years, I've visited and trained hundreds, maybe nearly a thousand operators in 911 centers across the country. Eight years of airports and rental cars. Eight years of system upgrades, launches, and long nights staring at glowing consoles in unfamiliar rooms.

But what stays with me isn't just the software. It's not the checklists or the seamless cutovers that keep the system running smoothly. It's the people. The quiet nods during briefings. The small talk that turns into whispered confessions when the room empties out. The laughter fills the spaces between the tones.

Behind every screen and blinking cursor, there's a story. A dispatcher who has endured three hurricanes. A trainee who just handled her first CPR call. A supervisor who hides his grief behind dark humor and a cup of cold coffee. While this work is about systems and stability, it's also about voices, the ones carrying the weight of someone else's worst day and those learning to find their own again.

My favorite moments in training aren't the big milestones. They're the quiet ones that almost go unnoticed. It's when a dispatcher pauses, works through the steps, and suddenly understands how to manually transfer a 911 call without their pulse spiking. You can see it in their posture, the shoulders drop, the grip on the mouse loosens, the breathing slows.

It sounds like a small skill, but it isn't. Those awkward, rarely used functions are what matter when everything else goes sideways. They're the difference between freezing and functioning when the system doesn't behave the way it should. That's the moment confidence replaces hesitation. Not because they memorized a process, but because they trust themselves. And for the first time, they realize they can stay steady when it actually counts.

It's never just about the technology. It's about restoring belief, belief that they can trust the tools, trust the training, and most of all, trust themselves. Their relief, their quiet "thank you," those moments when they feel seen and capable, that's where I find my purpose. That's when I know I'm exactly where I'm supposed to be.

Somewhere amidst the chaos of flights and center walls, I realized I was also rebuilding a part of myself. In the hum of a hotel air conditioner at midnight. In the rhythmic roll of tires on an unfamiliar highway. In the silence of an airport gate moments before boarding the next flight.

That's where healing was hidden, in the stillness I used to avoid. Every place I entered reflected back to me: reminders of who I used to be behind the headset, and glimpses of who I was becoming beyond it.

And hearing the welcome sound of his voice cutting through the noise: *"You're doing great. I'm proud of you."*

The country unfolded beneath me, vast and endless, each stop another dot on the map, another console glowing in a dim room, another set of faces etched with the lines of long shifts and quiet burdens. Every place had its own cadence, its own accent, its own way of carrying the work. And yet, everywhere I went, I met dispatchers who mirrored pieces of myself.

The younger me, eager but unsure, desperate to prove she belonged.

The weary me, so tired she couldn't feel her own exhaustion anymore.

The fractured me, stitched together after trauma, still healing, not yet whole.

From the window of a plane, I'd watch the country stretch wide beneath me, endless sweeps of green and gold stitched with rivers that shimmered like silver thread, roads curling like veins across the earth. And I'd remember: there was a time I forgot how to love it. How to love *any* of it. But somewhere between the takeoffs and landings, I began falling in love again, with the country, with the work, and with the life that was quietly, steadily forming around me.

Healing began in small, nearly invisible ways.

In the sigh I let out behind the wheel of a rental car in Wyoming, the kind that starts deep in your bones and leaves you hollowed out in the best way.

In a night of uninterrupted sleep in a quiet Oklahoma hotel, no phantom tones pulling me back to the console, just the comfort of knowing someone out there was keeping me in their thoughts.

In the unguarded smile that found me in a North Carolina center, when a dispatcher leaned over her coffee and whispered, *"I didn't think anyone understood... until today."*

I wasn't just training them.

They were saving me.

And so was he.

Somewhere between the skies and the glow of center consoles, I stumbled into something I hadn't even realized I was searching for: Peace. The kind that lets you finally set it down for a while. And Love, not the kind that hurts, tests, or evaporates when life gets hard, but the kind that stays. The kind that holds your mess in his hands and still calls it beautiful.

For the first time in years, I felt a sense of belonging. Not to a shift. Not to a title. Not even to the headset that had defined me. But to myself. And to someone who saw all of me, the scars, the fractures, the shadows, and stayed.

You can't fully explain this work to someone who hasn't experienced it. Not really. But maybe, through these pages, you'll catch a piece of it: the rhythm, the rewiring, the way it reshapes your nervous system and your soul. You learn to keep your voice calm when every nerve inside you is screaming. You train your hands to move while your heart absorbs someone else's chaos. Over the years, that voice behind the mic becomes your default.

For a long time, it became *me*. So much so that I forgot I had another voice.

This is my other voice. The one that doesn't have to stay composed. The one that can shake, and crack, and break into tears. The one that tells the truth, not the polished version, not the scripted protocol, but the story that lived beneath the uniform, beneath the headset, beneath the armor I wore for decades.

This is me. And if you've never felt seen in your storm, I hope this voice finds you and reminds you: you are not alone.

Healing, I realized, doesn't arrive with fanfare. It doesn't announce itself with clean breaks and tidy resolutions. It creeps in like a reintroduction to the future. Not a brand-new identity, but a reclaimed one. Sometimes it comes through the miles you've traveled and the lessons you've learned. And sometimes it comes through a person, someone who looks at you, battle-scarred and imperfect, still trembling, still healing, and says without hesitation, *"I'm not going anywhere."*

I wasn't just surviving anymore.

I was living.

And finally... I was living *Beyond the Headset.*

# Epilogue

These days, my world looks different.

Quieter. Simpler.

The tones and static of dispatch have been replaced with the soft bleating of goats, the bray of miniature donkeys, and the cluck of chickens greeting the morning.

Instead of twelve-hour shifts under fluorescent lights, I wake to Tennessee sunlight spilling across rolling fields and my husband by my side.

I still travel across the U.S. to teach and program 911 systems, and I love every moment of it. But now, I come home to this: a farm that grounds me, a husband who steadies me, and a peace I once thought I'd never deserve. I'm learning, day by day, about forgiveness, grace, and gratitude.

The farm isn't fancy; it isn't meant to be. It's peace in its most ordinary form: dirt under my nails, the sound of hooves in the pasture, the small joy of gathering fresh eggs from the coop. After years of chaos and broken sleep, I've found healing in the rhythm of chores and the steadiness of simple days.

This life wasn't handed to me; it was built, brick by brick, mile by mile, choice by choice. And in the building, I found more than rest. I found a partnership. I found a man who loves me not despite my scars, but through them, a love that steadies me when the past tries to pull me back.

When I stand at the fence line and watch the donkeys nudge each other playfully, or when I listen to the wind sweep across the hills at dusk, I realize this is what *beyond* truly means, beyond the headset, beyond the storms, beyond the years of carrying voices that weren't my own.

The world I live in now feels small in the best way: a farm, a husband who notices me, animals who rely on me, and a peace I once

208

thought was unreachable. It doesn't erase the past or undo the weight I carried, but it reminds me every day that survival isn't the end of the story. Life after survival can be beautiful, too. And here, on this patch of Tennessee soil, I finally let myself believe it. I let myself grow and slowed myself down enough to start *healing*.